The
COMPLETE
BABY
CHECKLIST

The COMPLETE BABY CHECKLIST

A Total Organizing System For Parents

ELYSE ZORN KARLIN, DAISY SPIER and MONA BRODY

Illustrated by Anne Cook

AVON BOOKS ▲ NEW YORK

This book is adapted from a collection previously self-published under the title The Best Baby Gift: A Total Organizing System for New Parents, copyright © 1988 by Summer House Publishers, Inc.

This book is not intended for the purpose of parental diagnosis or medical treatment of children. Parents of children with specific health concerns should discuss these concerns with their pediatricians. Before starting a child on any diet or eating program, or before changing or altering a doctor-prescribed eating program, parents should discuss the intended diet with their pediatricians. Although every effort has been made to include the most current information in this book, there can be no guarantee that this information won't change with time and further research.

AVON BOOKS
A division of
The Hearst Corporation
1350 Avenue of the Americas
New York, New York 10019

Text copyright © 1992 by Elyse Karlin, Daisy Spier and Mona Brody
Illustrations copyright © 1992 by Anne Cook
Cover art by Anne Cook
Published by arrangement with the authors
ISBN: 0-380-76347-8

First Avon Books Trade Printing: March 1992

AVON TRADEMARK REG. U. S. PAT. OFF. AND IN OTHER COUNTRIES, MARCA REGISTRADA, HECHO EN U.S.A

Printed in the U.S.A.

ARC 10 9 8 7 6 5 4 3 2

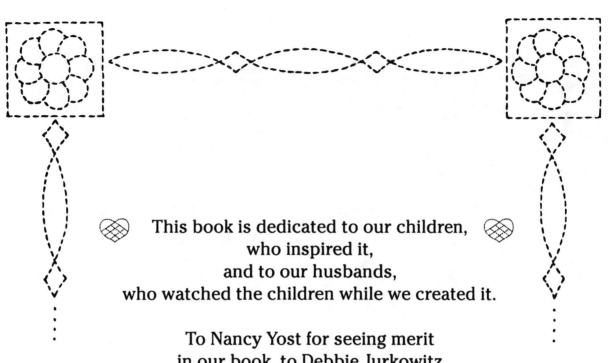

This book is dedicated to our children,
who inspired it,
and to our husbands,
who watched the children while we created it.

To Nancy Yost for seeing merit
in our book, to Debbie Jurkowitz
for her tremendous editing efforts,
to Jody Rein for seeing it through,
and to Dr. Stephen Boris.

CONTENTS

INTRODUCTION   XI

PART ONE: PREPARING FOR BABY'S ARRIVAL   1
   LAST-TRIMESTER CHECKLIST   5
   LAST-MONTH CHECKLIST   7
   LAYETTE CHECKLIST   9
   PREPARING THE NURSERY   11
   NAME WORKSHEET/FIRST NAME   12
   NAME WORKSHEET/MIDDLE NAME   13
   ANNOUNCEMENT LIST   14
   RELIGIOUS CEREMONY GUEST LIST   16
   GIFT/THANK YOU NOTE CHECKLIST   18
   HOSPITAL CHECKLIST   20
   HOSPITAL CALL LIST   22
   DAD'S CHECKLIST   24

PART TWO: BUYING EQUIPMENT AND CLOTHING   25
   EQUIPMENT CHECKLIST   29
   GUIDELINES FOR CHOOSING EQUIPMENT   31
   GUIDELINES FOR BUYING CHILDREN'S CLOTHING   37

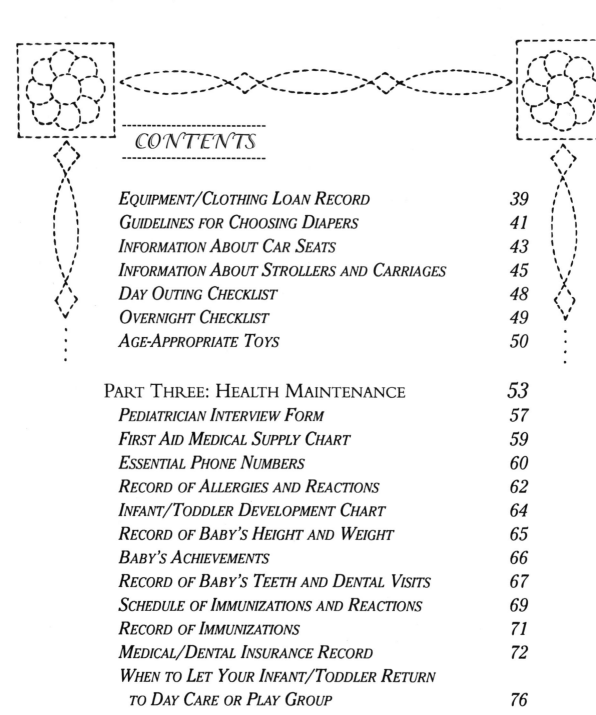

CONTENTS

EQUIPMENT/CLOTHING LOAN RECORD   39
GUIDELINES FOR CHOOSING DIAPERS   41
INFORMATION ABOUT CAR SEATS   43
INFORMATION ABOUT STROLLERS AND CARRIAGES 45
DAY OUTING CHECKLIST   48
OVERNIGHT CHECKLIST   49
AGE-APPROPRIATE TOYS   50

PART THREE: HEALTH MAINTENANCE   53
PEDIATRICIAN INTERVIEW FORM   57
FIRST AID MEDICAL SUPPLY CHART   59
ESSENTIAL PHONE NUMBERS   60
RECORD OF ALLERGIES AND REACTIONS   62
INFANT/TODDLER DEVELOPMENT CHART   64
RECORD OF BABY'S HEIGHT AND WEIGHT   65
BABY'S ACHIEVEMENTS   66
RECORD OF BABY'S TEETH AND DENTAL VISITS 67
SCHEDULE OF IMMUNIZATIONS AND REACTIONS   69
RECORD OF IMMUNIZATIONS   71
MEDICAL/DENTAL INSURANCE RECORD   72
WHEN TO LET YOUR INFANT/TODDLER RETURN
   TO DAY CARE OR PLAY GROUP   76

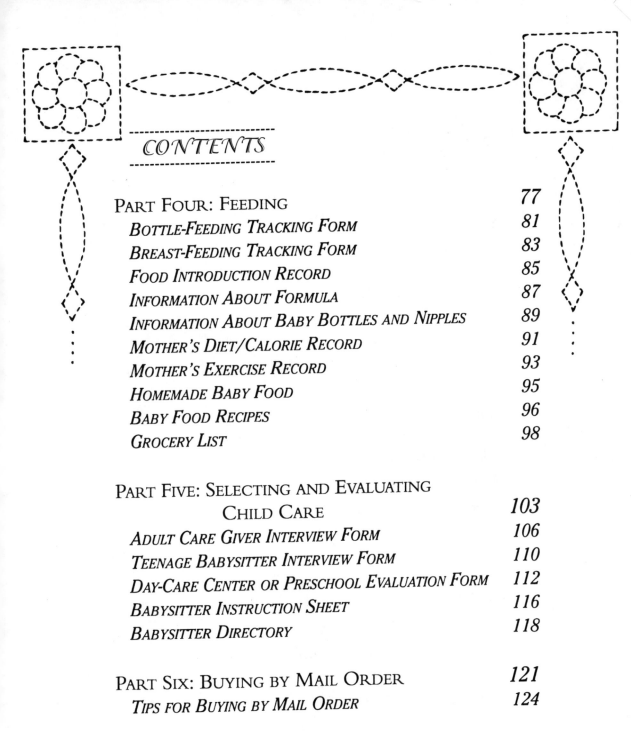

CONTENTS

PART FOUR: FEEDING   77
   BOTTLE-FEEDING TRACKING FORM   81
   BREAST-FEEDING TRACKING FORM   83
   FOOD INTRODUCTION RECORD   85
   INFORMATION ABOUT FORMULA   87
   INFORMATION ABOUT BABY BOTTLES AND NIPPLES   89
   MOTHER'S DIET/CALORIE RECORD   91
   MOTHER'S EXERCISE RECORD   93
   HOMEMADE BABY FOOD   95
   BABY FOOD RECIPES   96
   GROCERY LIST   98

PART FIVE: SELECTING AND EVALUATING CHILD CARE   103
   ADULT CARE GIVER INTERVIEW FORM   106
   TEENAGE BABYSITTER INTERVIEW FORM   110
   DAY-CARE CENTER OR PRESCHOOL EVALUATION FORM   112
   BABYSITTER INSTRUCTION SHEET   116
   BABYSITTER DIRECTORY   118

PART SIX: BUYING BY MAIL ORDER   121
   TIPS FOR BUYING BY MAIL ORDER   124

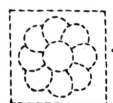

CONTENTS

MAIL-ORDER PURCHASING RECORD 125

MAIL-ORDER RESOURCES 127

   BABY ANNOUNCEMENTS 127

   BABY EQUIPMENT 128

   BOOKS AND CASSETTES ON PARENTING 131

   CHILDREN'S BOOKS 132

   CHILDREN'S CLOTHING 133

   CHILDREN'S FURNITURE 136

   CHILDREN'S LINENS 137

   CHILDREN'S MUSIC AND VIDEO 138

   GIFTS FOR EXPECTANT FAMILIES 140

   MATERNITY AND NURSING CLOTHES 141

   NURSING SUPPLIES 142

   TOYS AND EDUCATIONAL ITEMS 143

PART SEVEN: RESOURCES 147

   ORGANIZATIONS 150

   MAGAZINES AND NEWSLETTERS 156

   PARENTS' GROUPS AND PRESCHOOL
     ACTIVITIES RECORD 157

   CHILD'S FRIENDS AND PARENTS 159

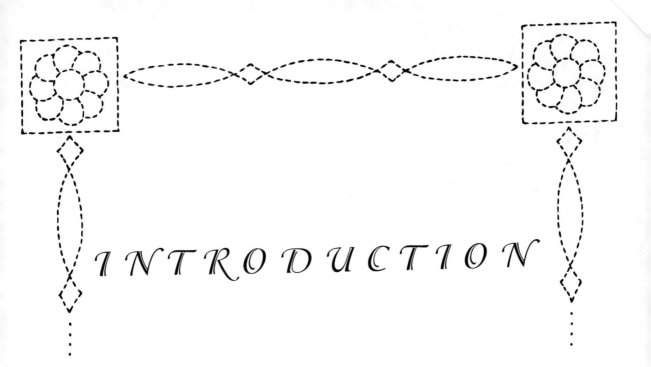

INTRODUCTION

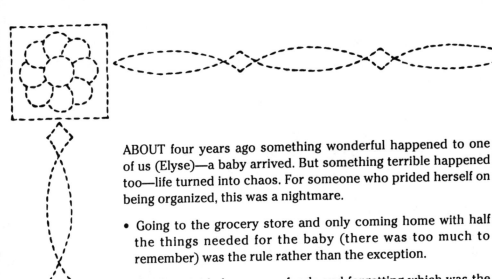

ABOUT four years ago something wonderful happened to one of us (Elyse)—a baby arrived. But something terrible happened too—life turned into chaos. For someone who prided herself on being organized, this was a nightmare.

- Going to the grocery store and only coming home with half the things needed for the baby (there was too much to remember) was the rule rather than the exception.

- Starting the baby on new foods and forgetting which was the most recent happened several times. When the baby developed a food allergy, there was no way to know which food caused it.

- Using the last diaper and discovering there were no more left was **awful!**

- Promising to return borrowed baby equipment, and clothing and then not remembering who lent it was frustrating.

- And most embarrassing was not being able to recall who had been sent a thank you note for a baby gift and who hadn't been sent one.

These experiences were certainly not unique. Most new mothers and fathers find lack of sleep and the constant demands of a new baby leave little time to do more than care for the baby—certainly no time to get organized.

It was clear to us that parents could use some help in this area. We set out to develop a practical system that would help expectant and new parents organize all the tasks and details in their lives that pregnancy and a baby bring.

We are happy to report that Elyse and her husband are now the calm parents of an almost-four-year-old child—and they didn't think they would survive the first year.

What happened? The baby began to sleep through the night, and we developed *The Complete Baby Checklist: A Total Orga-*

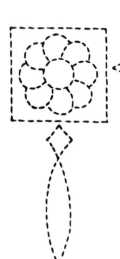

nizing System For Parents. Using these organizing forms and charts helped a lot, and we hope it's going to do the same for you.

How to Use The Complete Baby Checklist

This book is divided into seven sections. At the beginning of each section is a description of the organizing forms and charts and how to use them. Start by familiarizing yourself with each of the sections. If you're awaiting baby's arrival, you can start using Part One immediately, and parts of some of the other sections as well. If you do, you'll have a head start on being organized when baby arrives.

Some of the forms in this book are intended for use outside the home. In most cases you can just take this book with you and use the forms right in the book. However, for some forms, such as the grocery shopping list, which you'll want to use over and over again, it might be wise to make some photocopies so you'll have unlimited usage. We think the forms and list are helpful as they are, but everybody is different. So feel free to change or adapt them to suit your needs.

Keep the book in a handy place so it is accessible to everyone who will take care of baby—Mom, Dad, care giver, grandparents, and so forth. Try keeping it in the kitchen, or in the room where you spend the most time.

The Complete Baby Checklist is primarily meant to be used from the end of your pregnancy throughout the first year of baby's life. However, many of the forms will continue to be useful through the preschool years. Simply refer to the Contents to find the help you need.

Elyse Zorn Karlin, Daisy Spier, Mona Brody

PART ONE

Preparing for Baby's Arrival

THE last trimester of pregnancy passes quickly. Suddenly you realize that there's a lot to do before the baby is born. The same is true if you're awaiting a baby through adoption.

To help you feel more organized in preparing for baby's arrival, we've created a number of checklists for Mom and Dad. Of course, many items included are subject to personal preference. You certainly don't have to buy or do *everything* on these lists, but they should be helpful in making certain nothing important is forgotten:

LAST-TRIMESTER CHECKLIST
Includes items that require lead time to order, do, or select.

LAST-MONTH CHECKLIST
Covers those last-minute details you may forget as you become excited and anxious about baby's arrival.

LAYETTE CHECKLIST
This is a list of the basic items of clothing and linens you'll need for your new baby. We've used minimum amounts here. If you want to do laundry less often, you can opt to buy more, but keep in mind how quickly babies outgrow their clothes.

PREPARING THE NURSERY
Here's everything you need for baby's room.

NAME WORKSHEETS
During the months that you are waiting for baby, jot down your favorite names, and narrow the list down to your first choice.

ANNOUNCEMENT LIST
You'll be too busy to draw up an announcement list after baby arrives, so do it beforehand if you can.

RELIGIOUS CEREMONY GUEST LIST
If you're planning to have a christening or bris, you should plan your guest list before baby is born. Select guests from your announcement list.

GIFT/THANK YOU NOTE CHECKLIST

It's wonderful—there are baby showers before, and visitors bearing gifts after. But you're so tired and busy, it's difficult to remember who gave which gift and whether or not you sent a thank you note. Use this list to avoid embarrassing errors.

HOSPITAL CHECKLIST

The last thing you want to do is to start looking for all these things to take with you when you go into labor. Pack two to four weeks before your due date.

HOSPITAL CALL LIST

Names and numbers will help Mom and Dad remember to call everyone and keep track of who has not been reached with the happy news of baby's arrival.

DAD'S CHECKLIST

Dad has a lot to do while Mom is in the hospital. This list will help him remember everything.

LAST-TRIMESTER CHECKLIST

❑ **B**egin buying layette. If you're uncomfortable with having these items at home in advance, many stores will hold them aside for you.

❑ **S**ign up for childbirth classes. Ask your doctor or hospital for recommendations. Investigate Bradley versus Lamaze method.

❑ **C**heck insurance coverage for well-baby care and your own hospitalization. Many insurance companies now insist they be notified in advance.

❑ **S**tart looking at baby announcements.

❑ **T**hink about buying a good camera if you don't have one. Keep in mind that some hospitals forbid the use of flashes in the delivery room, and choose your camera accordingly.

❑ **S**tart looking through mail-order catalogs for any items you might want to order.

❑ **R**ead about breast-feeding and be prepared for any problems. You may also want to discuss it with your doctor or attend a few meetings of the La Leche League, an organization that promotes breast-feeding. There should be a local chapter in your area.

❑ **A**rrange details of your maternity leave with your employer.

❑ **R**egister with hospital/birthing center where you will deliver baby. Some doctors may do this for you on request.

❑ Discuss your anesthesia options with an anesthesiologist at the hospital.

❑ Interview pediatricians. (See the forms in Part Three.)

❑ Start thinking of child-care options. You might want to make some calls and begin interviewing care givers or visiting day-care centers.

☒ Begin painting, wallpapering, and carpeting baby's room. As exhausting as this may seem now, it will be more difficult to do once baby is here.

❑ Find out which pieces of baby equipment and/or furniture friends and relatives will lend or give you. (See "Preparing the Nursery" checklist and "Equipment" checklists.) Order nursery furniture, custom quilts, and curtains early.

❑ Explore diaper services. Compare prices, and check on frequency of delivery/pickup as well as options for cloth versus disposables.

❑ If there are other children in the family, by now you have probably told them about the new baby. It's a good time to buy a book for siblings that discusses being a big brother or sister, and to check with your hospital to see if there are any special "sibling" classes to help prepare the older child for the baby and Mom's hospital stay. You might also have siblings help decorate and select items for baby's room.

6

LAST-MONTH CHECKLIST

☒ Start addressing announcement envelopes. It will save you precious time later.

❑ Pay bills as they come in and keep correspondence up-to-date. You'll be surprised how fast this piles up after baby arrives.

❑ Spend time having fun with dad-to-be. Go out to dinner, movies, etc., as often as you can.

❑ Rest and pamper yourself as much as possible. Now's the time to rent your favorite video, read that book you've always wanted to, and put your feet up.

☒ Pack your suitcase for the hospital; include clothes for baby.

☒ Begin reading books on care of new babies.

☒ Make list of people to call about baby's birth. (See "Hospital Call List.")

❑ Cook double portions of meals and freeze them.

☒ Buy a supply of: diapers, cotton balls, cotton swabs, bottles, pacifiers, baby wipes, baby soap, baby shampoo, baby powder, petroleum jelly, diaper ointment.

☒ Buy nursing pads, sanitary napkins, Preparation H, Tucks (antiseptic pads), for your postpartum return.

LAST-MONTH CHECKLIST

❑ Make arrangements for help after the birth of your baby. Check with family and friends, or arrange for a baby nurse if you're planning to have one.

❑ Pre-wash all the baby's clothes and linens with baby soap or detergent, e.g., Ivory Snow or Dreft.

❑ Make a final decision about names.

❑ Decide where baby will sleep when coming home from the hospital. Some parents prefer to keep the baby in their room for the first few weeks.

❑ Discuss circumcision with your doctor or religious leader and get recommendations and references from friends.

❑ Take sibling to buy a gift for the new baby; and buy one for the sibling to get after the baby is born. Some parents like to say it's a gift from the new baby.

❑ Check if hospital will allow siblings to visit the new baby.

❑ Decide who will watch the sibling while Mom's in the hospital, and have a backup plan in case labor is early or your first choice becomes unavailable.

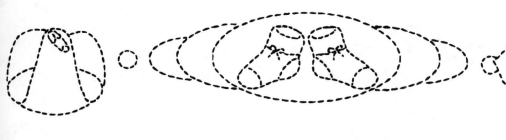

LAYETTE CHECKLIST

- ❑ "Coming home from the hospital" outfit: something comfortable for baby to wear. In cold weather, also bring a bunting or heavy blanket. In warmer weather you may just need a light blanket.
- ❑ Undershirts (4–7); Onesies or other snap-crotch type recommended because they do not ride up on baby.
- ❑ Flame-retardant stretchies or pajamas (4–7)
- ❑ Kimonos/nightgowns (4–7)
- ❑ Other "dressier" outfits for visitors or special outings (3–5)
- ❑ Hooded towels and washcloths (3)
- ❑ Receiving blankets (3–5)
- ❑ Quilts (2)
- ❑ Crib sheets (3)
- ❑ Bumpers for crib
- ❑ Flannel-covered rubber sheets (2–3)
- ❑ Changing table covers (3)

9

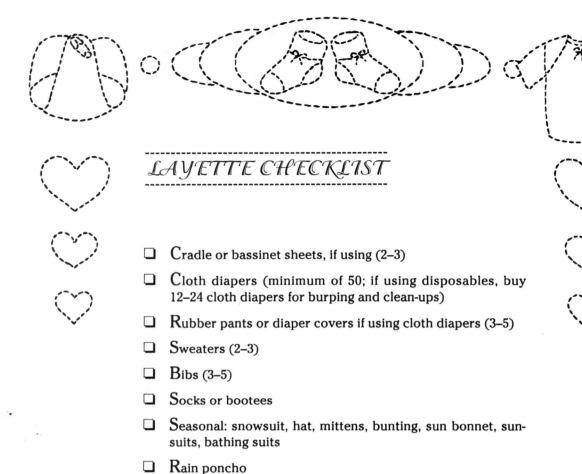

LAYETTE CHECKLIST

- ❏ Cradle or bassinet sheets, if using (2–3)
- ❏ Cloth diapers (minimum of 50; if using disposables, buy 12–24 cloth diapers for burping and clean-ups)
- ❏ Rubber pants or diaper covers if using cloth diapers (3–5)
- ❏ Sweaters (2–3)
- ❏ Bibs (3–5)
- ❏ Socks or bootees
- ❏ Seasonal: snowsuit, hat, mittens, bunting, sun bonnet, sun-suits, bathing suits
- ❏ Rain poncho

PREPARING THE NURSERY

- ❑ Dresser
- ❑ Temporary bed or bassinet
- ☒ Rocking chair
- ❑ Crib
- ❑ Hamper
- ❑ Quilt and bumpers
- ❑ Lamp/night light/dimmer
- ❑ Diaper pail
- ❑ Music box
- ❑ Stain-proof carpeting
- ❑ Humidifier

- ☒ Baby nail scissors or clippers
- ☒ Baby wipes
- ❑ Baby powder
- ❑ Diaper cream
- ❑ Cotton balls
- ❑ Changing table
- ❑ Thermometer
- ❑ Nasal aspirator
- ☒ Clock
- ☒ Baby comb and brush
- ❑ Nursery monitor/intercom

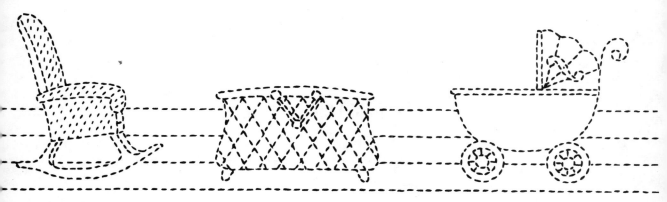

ITS A BOY! ✿ ITS A GIRL!

NAME WORKSHEET— FIRST NAME

TOP TEN CHOICES

BOY	GIRL
1.	
2.	
3.	
4.	
5.	
6.	
7.	
8.	
9.	
10.	

THREE FINAL CHOICES

1.	
2.	
3.	

FINAL CHOICE

LBS.

OZ.

IT'S A BOY! ✿ IT'S A GIRL!

LBS.

NAME WORKSHEET—
MIDDLE NAME

TOP TEN CHOICES

BOY	GIRL
1.	
2.	
3.	
4.	
5.	
6.	
7.	
8.	
9.	
10.	

THREE FINAL CHOICES

1.	
2.	
3.	

FINAL CHOICE

IT'S A BOY! IT'S A GIRL!

ANNOUNCEMENT LIST

NAME	ADDRESS	DATE SENT
_____	_____	_____
_____	_____	_____
_____	_____	_____
_____	_____	_____
_____	_____	_____
_____	_____	_____
_____	_____	_____
_____	_____	_____
_____	_____	_____
_____	_____	_____
_____	_____	_____

LBS.

IT'S A BOY! ❀ IT'S A GIRL!

LBS.

OZ.

ANNOUNCEMENT LIST

NAME	ADDRESS	DATE SENT

RELIGIOUS CEREMONY
GUEST LIST*

NAME	RELATIONSHIP	DATE CALLED	ATTENDING YES	NO
¹ GRANDMA O			☐	☐
¹ PA O			☐	☐
¹ GRANDPA P			☐	☐
¹ Jennifer O			☐	☐
¹ JON BLOOD			☐	☐
5 PREINER Family			☐	☐
4 Tom + Julie Palach			☐	☐
2 Jack + Nettie Palach			☐	☐
¹ Great GRANDPA KASTNER			☐	☐
¹ DENNY KASTNER			☐	☐
¹ Nicole KASTNER			☐	☐
¹ BRENT KASTNER			☐	☐
¹ Jill Jekot			☐	☐
			☐	☐
			☐	☐
			☐	☐
			☐	☐
			☐	☐
			☐	☐
			☐	☐

*This form can be used for a christening, bris, other religious ceremonies, or for a nonreligious celebration of baby's birth.

16

RELIGIOUS CEREMONY GUEST LIST*

NAME	RELATIONSHIP	DATE CALLED	ATTENDING YES	NO
			❑	❑
			❑	❑
			❑	❑
			❑	❑
			❑	❑
			❑	❑
			❑	❑
			❑	❑
			❑	❑
			❑	❑
			❑	❑
			❑	❑
			❑	❑
			❑	❑
			❑	❑
			❑	❑
			❑	❑
			❑	❑
			❑	❑
			❑	❑

*This form can be used for a christening, bris, other religious ceremonies, or for a nonreligious celebration of baby's birth.

GIFT/THANK YOU NOTE CHECKLIST

DESCRIBE GIFT	FROM	DATE RECEIVED	NOTE SENT
			☐
			☐
			☐
			☐
			☐
			☐
			☐
			☐
			☐
			☐
			☐
			☐
			☐
			☐
			☐
			☐
			☐
			☐
			☐

GIFT/THANK YOU NOTE CHECKLIST

DESCRIBE GIFT	FROM	DATE RECEIVED	NOTE SENT
			☐
			☐
			☐
			☐
			☐
			☐
			☐
			☐
			☐
			☐
			☐
			☐
			☐
			☐
			☐
			☐
			☐
			☐
			☐
			☐

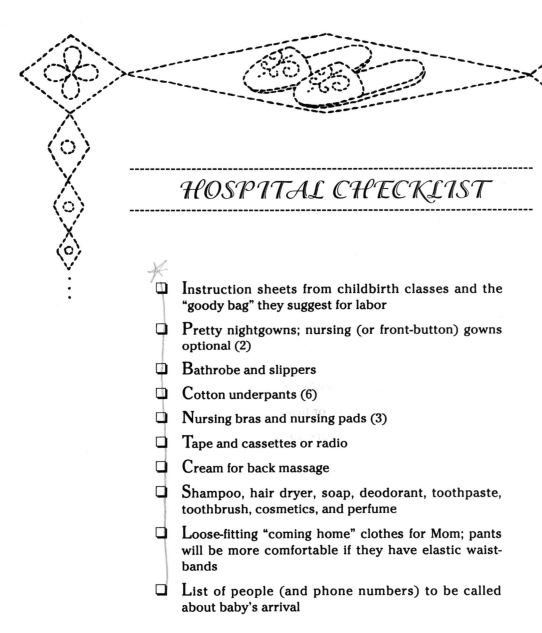

HOSPITAL CHECKLIST

- ❑ Instruction sheets from childbirth classes and the "goody bag" they suggest for labor
- ❑ Pretty nightgowns; nursing (or front-button) gowns optional (2)
- ❑ Bathrobe and slippers
- ❑ Cotton underpants (6)
- ❑ Nursing bras and nursing pads (3)
- ❑ Tape and cassettes or radio
- ❑ Cream for back massage
- ❑ Shampoo, hair dryer, soap, deodorant, toothpaste, toothbrush, cosmetics, and perfume
- ❑ Loose-fitting "coming home" clothes for Mom; pants will be more comfortable if they have elastic waistbands
- ❑ List of people (and phone numbers) to be called about baby's arrival

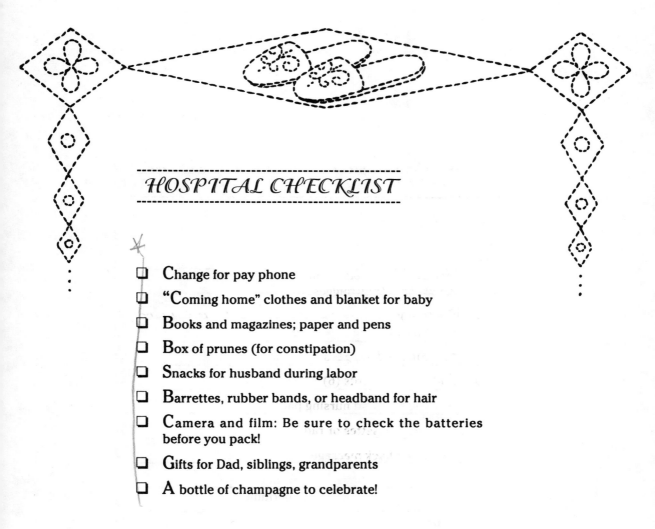

HOSPITAL CHECKLIST

- ❑ Change for pay phone
- ❑ "Coming home" clothes and blanket for baby
- ❑ Books and magazines; paper and pens
- ❑ Box of prunes (for constipation)
- ❑ Snacks for husband during labor
- ❑ Barrettes, rubber bands, or headband for hair
- ❑ Camera and film: Be sure to check the batteries before you pack!
- ❑ Gifts for Dad, siblings, grandparents
- ❑ A bottle of champagne to celebrate!

21

HOSPITAL CALL LIST

NAME	RELATIONSHIP	PHONE #	REACHED
		PAGER - 527-3095	
		DAD W - 337-2092	
Grandma + GRANDPA	ORTZER	H-475-0606	☐
GRANDPA PALACH		1-512-581-0636	☐
GREAT-GPA KASTNER		522-8915	☐
PREINERS		1-218-749-8164	☐
PALACH'S (Tom+Julie)		H-229-2669 W-229-2234	☐
PalAch's (Jack+Nettie)		715-344-7139	☐
Bill Chesney	H-475-2583	W-420-1445	☐
H P'- Tom Simansky			☐
MARY + Ty ARMSTRONG		942-0462	☐
Jennifer	AUNT	727-7411	☐
			☐
			☐
Mom- Call Linda K.			☐
			☐
			☐
			☐
			☐
			☐
			☐
			☐
			☐

22

HOSPITAL CALL LIST

NAME	RELATIONSHIP	PHONE #	REACHED
Julie Call			☐
— Joyce			☐
— Teresa			☐
— Desiree			☐
— Robin			☐
— Molly W			☐
— Michelle			☐
— Katie Johnson			☐
			☐
			☐
			☐
			☐
			☐
			☐
			☐
			☐
			☐
			☐
			☐
			☐
			☐

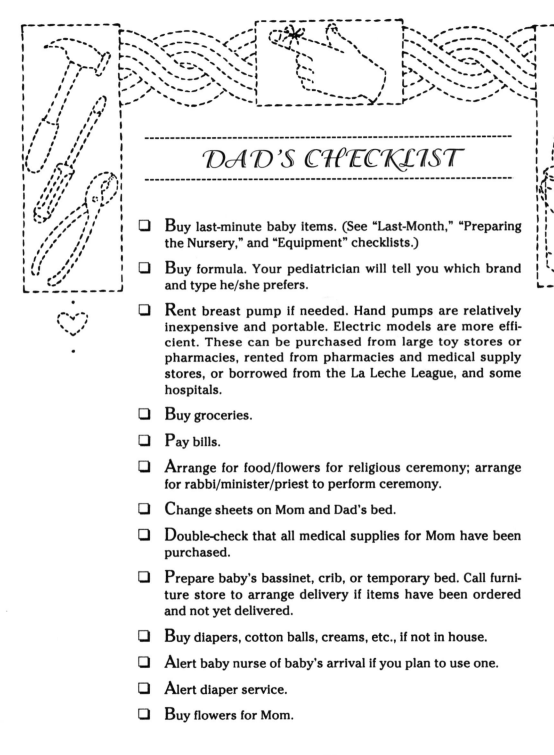

DAD'S CHECKLIST

❑ Buy last-minute baby items. (See "Last-Month," "Preparing the Nursery," and "Equipment" checklists.)

❑ Buy formula. Your pediatrician will tell you which brand and type he/she prefers.

❑ Rent breast pump if needed. Hand pumps are relatively inexpensive and portable. Electric models are more efficient. These can be purchased from large toy stores or pharmacies, rented from pharmacies and medical supply stores, or borrowed from the La Leche League, and some hospitals.

❑ Buy groceries.

❑ Pay bills.

❑ Arrange for food/flowers for religious ceremony; arrange for rabbi/minister/priest to perform ceremony.

❑ Change sheets on Mom and Dad's bed.

❑ Double-check that all medical supplies for Mom have been purchased.

❑ Prepare baby's bassinet, crib, or temporary bed. Call furniture store to arrange delivery if items have been ordered and not yet delivered.

❑ Buy diapers, cotton balls, creams, etc., if not in house.

❑ Alert baby nurse of baby's arrival if you plan to use one.

❑ Alert diaper service.

❑ Buy flowers for Mom.

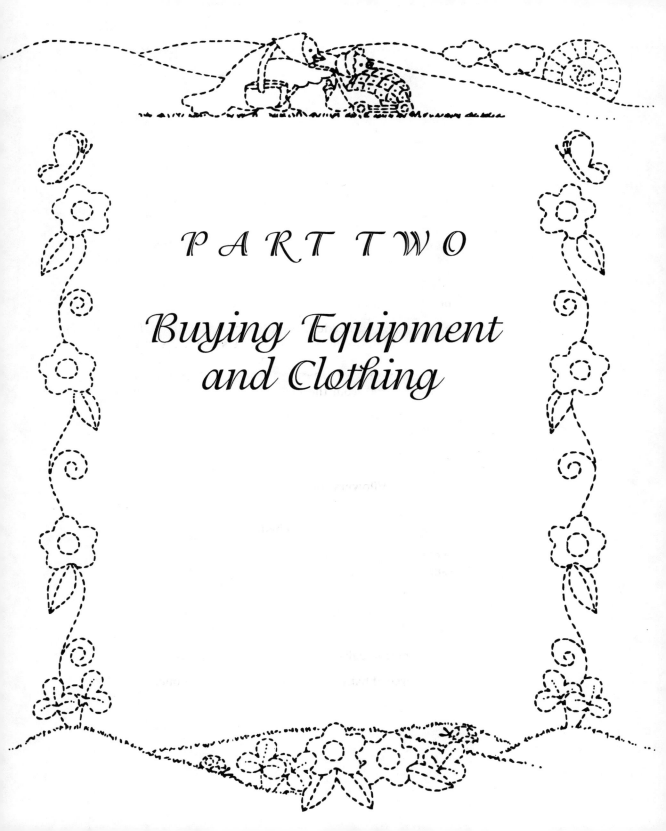

PART TWO

Buying Equipment and Clothing

THERE'S so much baby paraphernalia available today that it's sometimes difficult to know which to choose and what's really necessary to have. These lists are designed to provide you with information about the type of equipment and clothing you'll need for baby and to offer guidelines on how to select these items. There are also two travel checklists of all the basic essentials to have on hand when going out with baby, and a special chart on toys for the first year.

EQUIPMENT CHECKLIST

Details the basic equipment you'll need. You certainly don't have to buy all these things before the baby arrives, but this will also help you in asking your friends and relatives to give or lend you equipment they no longer are using.

GUIDELINES FOR CHOOSING EQUIPMENT

Provides information on what to look for when buying a crib, walker, playpen, high chair, and other basic items. Equipment that does not meet government and industry standards can be *dangerous*. The purchasing information in this checklist is very important to ensure your child's safety.

GUIDELINES FOR BUYING CHILDREN'S CLOTHING

Suggests what to look for in fabric, construction, and design—this can increase the durability and longevity of baby's clothes.

EQUIPMENT/CLOTHING LOAN RECORD

Friends and relatives will probably be lending you baby equipment and clothes. Some will want the items returned, and some won't. As time goes on, you won't remember which item came from which person. When you borrow something, list it here immediately, and you'll really appreciate that you did when it's time to return it.

GUIDELINES FOR CHOOSING DIAPERS

Explains all the options and various types available from cloth to disposables.

INFORMATION ABOUT CAR SEATS

Car seats are one of the most important pieces of equipment you can buy to protect your baby. This chart will help you make a decision on which is the best type for your child.

INFORMATION ABOUT STROLLERS AND CARRIAGES

There are so many different types of strollers and carriages, you can easily choose the wrong kind because you aren't aware of all your options. This information may help you get it right on the first try.

DAY OUTING CHECKLIST

Includes everything you'll need for a normal day out with baby, whether for a few hours or all day.

OVERNIGHT CHECKLIST

Provides a list of the additional items you'll need if you'll be away from home one night or more.

AGE-APPROPRIATE TOYS

This will give you an idea of the kinds of toys to buy your child. Remember, every child is different in development and preferences.

EQUIPMENT CHECKLIST

FOR IMMEDIATE USE:

- ❑ Infant car seat
- ☒ "Doughnut" cushion for baby's head in car seat
- ❑ Baby carrier
- ❑ Infant seat or baby rocker
- ❑ Diaper bag
- ❑ Combination folding travel bed/changing pad
- ❑ Bottles and bottle brush (if not breast-feeding)
- ❑ Sterilizer or nipple rack for dishwasher
- ❑ Plastic, foam rubber, or inflatable baby bath
- ☒ "Baby shade" for car to block the sun
- ❑ Swinging cradle/bassinet
- ❑ Stroller/carriage
- ❑ Pacifiers (if baby likes)
- ❑ Mobiles
- ❑ Crib

EQUIPMENT CHECKLIST

WITHIN SIX MONTHS:

- ❑ Toys for teething
- ❑ Playpen
- ❑ Windup or electric swing
- ❑ Jolly Jumper or other suspension-type baby exerciser
- ❑ High chair or chair that attaches to table
- ❑ Safety gates, latches, electric outlet covers
- ❑ Car seat for bigger baby
- ❑ Walker
- ❑ Toy chest

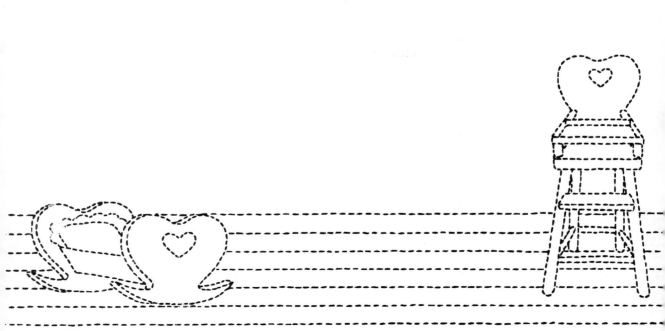

GUIDELINES FOR CHOOSING EQUIPMENT

CRIBS

❑ Mattress fits snugly; mattress height can be adjusted as child grows

❑ As large a distance as possible between the top side of the rail and the mattress so your child can't climb out

❑ Corner posts are flush with headboard or footboard so child's head or hands can't get stuck

❑ Corner posts should be less than ⅝ inch in height

❑ Space between slats is no wider than 2 ⅜ inches

❑ Stable, solid construction

❑ Locks on the drop side must lock securely every time side is raised and lowered

❑ Both sides of crib can be lowered

❑ Lowering mechanism is easy to use

❑ Plastic teething guards on top rails

❑ Nonlead paint used on crib

❑ Check to see if crib converts to junior bed; you may want this feature

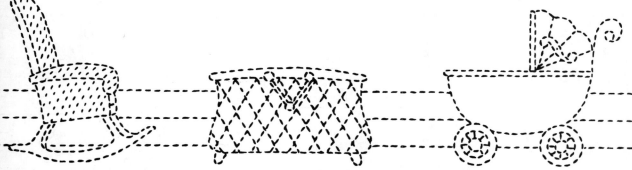

CHOOSING EQUIPMENT

BASSINETS AND CRADLES

❑ Sturdy bottom

❑ Wide, stable base so it is not easily tipped over

❑ Can accommodate standard-size bassinet mattress pads and sheets

BUMPER PADS

❑ Fit around whole crib

❑ Tie or snap in place

❑ Have at least six straps

❑ Surface is washable or has removable washable covers

BABY GATES

❑ Mesh gates are safer than accordion style, but make certain the mesh gates have small holes and do not have any sharp edges on mesh area or metal

❑ If gates have vertical slats, they should be no more than 2 ⅜ inches apart

❑ Avoid hinged joints that can pinch, and sharp hardware and small parts that can break off

❑ Permanent gates are sturdier than portable ones

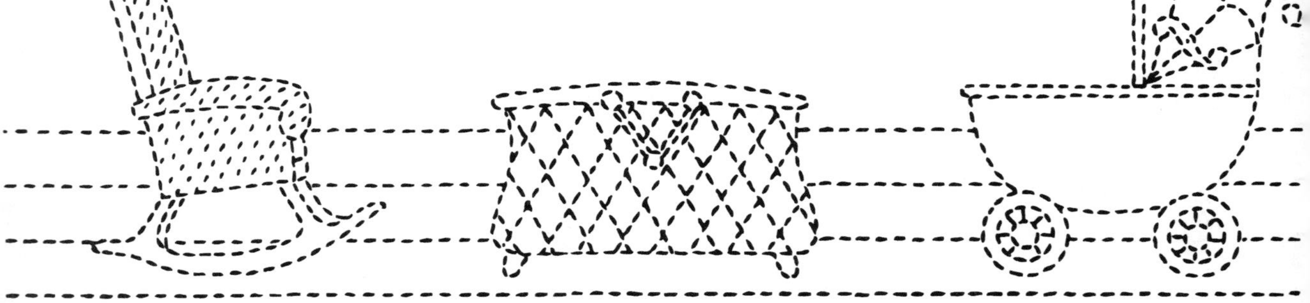

CHOOSING EQUIPMENT

HIGH CHAIRS

❑ Wide base for stability

❑ If chair has wheels, make sure wheels can lock

❑ Sturdy and easy-to-use safety straps

❑ Tray can be removed with one hand

❑ Splash-guard rim to prevent plates from falling off

❑ Easy to wash: Plastic trays are easiest to clean, as are plastic or vinyl seats

❑ Some high chairs are collapsible; check to see if this is easy to do

❑ Some newer models have adjustable seat heights

❑ Some high chairs convert to a table and chair

WALKERS

❑ Wide wheel base for stability

❑ Plastic sleeves over coil springs for safety

❑ No sharp metal edges

❑ Adjustable to baby's height

❑ Large tray for playing

Note: Some pediatricians are opposed to the use of walkers. Check with yours before buying.

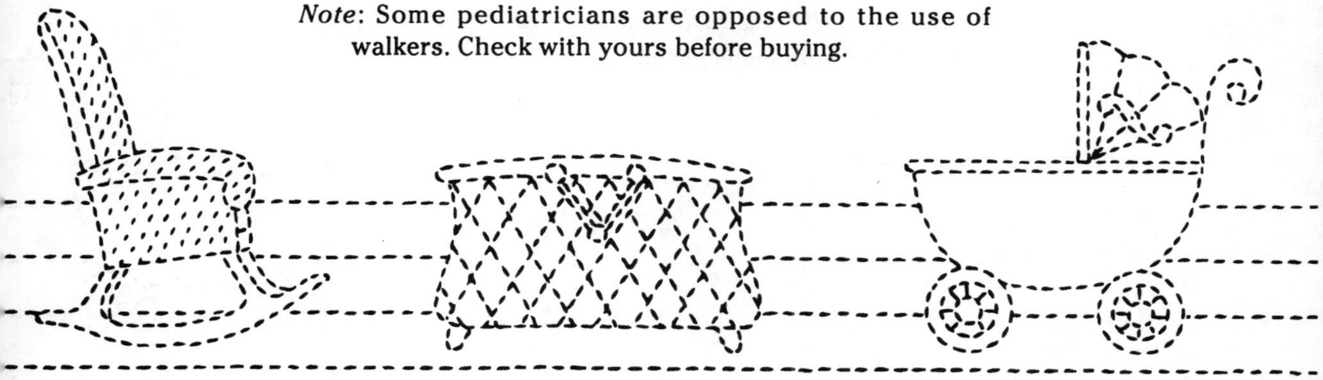

PLAYPENS

- ❑ Mesh netting with a very small weave: 2 ⅜ inches in width maximum

- ❑ Easy to open and close; hinges that lock tightly and will not open accidently

- ❑ Bottom pad should extend to edge of playpen and should be sturdy and easy to clean

TOY CHEST

- ❑ Hinges on lid should have support locks to hold lid in open position

- ❑ Ventilation holes that will not be blocked if chest is put against wall

FRONT AND BACK BABY CARRIERS

Carriers allow you to carry the baby without using your arms. Front carriers have straps that go over your shoulders, and sling carriers generally rest on your hips. Back carriers, generally not intended for use with newborns, resemble knapsacks (including metal frame). Each type uses a different set of muscles. Try it with baby and purchase the carrier that is most comfortable for you. Some carriers to investigate are: Sara's Ride, Snugli, Gerry, Lookabout, and the original Baby Sling.

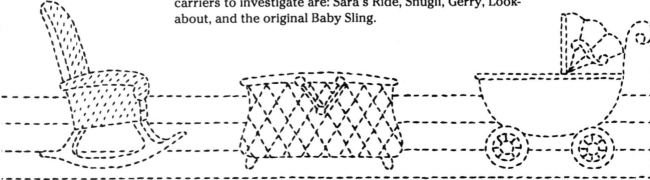

CHOOSING EQUIPMENT

Check for the following:

- ☐ Lightweight, sturdy, machine-washable fabric
- ☐ Padded shoulder straps
- ☐ Match baby's weight and length to manufacturer's weight and length limits
- ☐ Padded covering over metal frame near baby's face
- ☐ Head and neck support for baby
- ☐ Leg openings that won't allow baby to slide out but that will be comfortable
- ☐ Removable bib
- ☐ Storage pouches
- ☐ Easy to get on or off

PACIFIERS

- ☐ Strong enough not to come apart: One-piece construction is best
- ☐ Guard or shield must be large enough not to fit in baby's throat
- ☐ Shield must have ventilation holes
- ☐ Has no ribbon or string attached
- ☐ Some are orthodontically correct
- ☐ Your baby may prefer one type over another

BABY ROCKERS/INFANT SEATS

There are two basic types: One is made of molded plastic and has a handle so you can carry baby in it. The other is made of cloth which is stretched across a metal frame, and cannot be used as a carrier.

Plastic:

- ❑ Wide, sturdy base

- ❑ Nonskid feet

- ❑ Easy-to-use safety belt

- ❑ Easy-to-hold carrying handle

- ❑ Angle of back can be adjusted

- ❑ Optional rocking position

- ❑ Adequate padding; removable, washable padding

Cloth:

- ❑ Cloth seat conforms to baby's shape and weight

- ❑ Sturdy base and washable fabric

- ❑ Follow manufacturer's age and weight recommendations

Note: Additional variations are being produced; look for the same safety features.

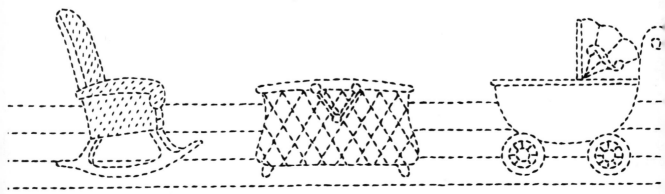

GUIDELINES FOR BUYING CHILDREN'S CLOTHING

DESIGN

- ❑ Snaps at bottom for ease of diapering
- ❑ Adjustments for growth that add life to garment (adjustable shoulder straps, elastic inserts)
- ❑ Wide seams
- ❑ Undefined waistlines in one-piece garment
- ❑ If item is two-piece, look for longer tops (won't ride up)
- ❑ Tucks, pleats, and yokes to give longer life to the item
- ❑ Not difficult to put over child's head, legs, and arms
- ❑ Designs that won't trip child
- ❑ Elastic waistbands
- ❑ Dolman sleeves

FABRICS

- ❑ Natural fibers (exception: buy acrylic instead of wool), either firmly woven or closely knit; soft and absorbent
- ❑ Machine washable
- ❑ No ironing required
- ❑ Bright colors for visibility

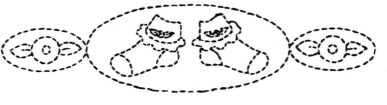

BUYING CHILDREN'S CLOTHING

SIZING

- ❑ Go by height and weight, not by size or age

- ❑ Room for normal growth—item won't be too small within a very short period of time (opt for larger over smaller)

- ❑ Enough room in crotch for child to move around

- ❑ Neck, waist, and sleeves are not too tight

Note: Infants sizes are 3 months, 6-9 months, 12 months, 18 months, 24 months (sometimes expressed in pounds also). Toddlers are 2T–4T, girls 4–6X, and boys 4–7.

EQUIPMENT/CLOTHING LOAN RECORD *

ITEM	FROM	CONDITION	TO BE RETURNED YES	NO
2 Tops + 2 skirts	Molly Lyons		☒	☐
			☐	☐
Bag of cloths, 1 top, + 1 dress			☒	☐ Nancy
			☐	☐
Dress + Books	Teresa Donnelly		☒	☐
			☐	☐
1 Blue Dress — Joyce			☐	☐
			☐	☐
			☐	☐
			☐	☐
			☐	☐
			☐	☐
			☐	☐
			☐	☐
			☐	☐
			☐	☐
			☐	☐
			☐	☐
			☐	☐

*Keep in mind that older cribs, car seats, and other equipment may not fit current federal safety guidelines. Check all borrowed equipment carefully for safety.

EQUIPMENT/CLOTHING LOAN RECORD *

ITEM	FROM	CONDITION	TO BE RETURNED	
			YES	NO
_____			☐	☐
_____			☐	☐
_____			☐	☐
_____			☐	☐
_____			☐	☐
_____			☐	☐
_____			☐	☐
_____			☐	☐
_____			☐	☐
_____			☐	☐
_____			☐	☐
_____			☐	☐
_____			☐	☐
_____			☐	☐
_____			☐	☐
_____			☐	☐
_____			☐	☐
_____			☐	☐

*Keep in mind that older cribs, car seats, and other equipment may not fit current federal safety guidelines. Check all borrowed equipment carefully for safety.

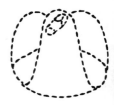

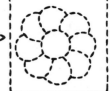

GUIDELINES FOR CHOOSING DIAPERS

DISPOSABLE DIAPERS

- Made of paper and special absorbent ingredients, and have a plastic outer cover.

- Available in a variety of brands, size, absorbencies, and prices.

  Read boxes carefully and choose the size that is appropriate for your baby's weight—small, medium, large, or extra-large. Some new diapers are sized according to baby's development—newborn, infant, crawler, and walker.

  Larger packages are more economical than the smaller ones. Store brands are less expensive than name brands.

  Main brands are Luvs, Huggies, and Pampers. See which brand fits and works best on your baby.

  All major brands now have diapers specifically designed for girls or boys. They have extra padding in strategic locations based on anatomical differences.

- Some manufacturers produce biodegradable diapers that are also disposable. These are sometimes more expensive.

- Disposable diapers may be more conducive to diaper rash because they are made of synthetic materials and do not "breathe."

CLOTH DIAPERS

- Most are made of woven cotton, though some are made of terry cloth and brushed flannel cotton.

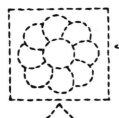

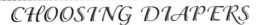

CHOOSING DIAPERS

- Most come in rectangular shapes that must be folded. Originally diaper pins were used to secure them, but now many diapers (Aware and Boomers) have Velcro attached. There are now some brands that are gathered at the legs.

- Most must be used with rubber pants or diaper covers (usually Velcro) to hold moisture in. (Bumpkins have a waterproof outer shell, so no diaper covers are necessary.)

- May be less likely to lead to diaper rash than disposables.

- Even if you use a diaper service, these are less expensive in the long run than disposables.

- Must be changed more frequently unless you double them or buy diaper linings.

DIAPER COVERS

- Plastic pants.

- Decorative cloth pants lined with plastic, cotton or unlined.

- You can use a Velcro or snap-closed diaper cover to hold regular diapers in place.

- These covers are available in a variety of prints and designs.

- Come in different sizes based on weight and age.

- Can be washed at home or sent to diaper service.

TRAINING PANTS

- Very absorbent underpants, usually with extra padding in the crotch area.

- Are usually terry cloth or cotton.

- Disposable paper ones have recently entered the market. These are like disposable diapers in the shape of pants.

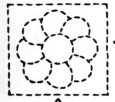

INFORMATION ABOUT CAR SEATS

INFANT-ONLY CAR SEATS

• Designed to be used in rear position only

• Used from birth to twenty pounds (with some exceptions)

• May have a variety of features, including:
    Two- or four-position recline
    Adjustable sun shield
    Removable tray
    Rocker base
    Carrying handles to remove seat and use as baby carrier
        or to affix to shopping cart
    Cloth or vinyl covers
    Swivel base to allow you to put baby in more easily

INFANT/TODDLER CAR SEAT

• Designed to be used in rear position for infants and forward
  for toddlers

• Used from birth to forty pounds (with some exceptions)

• May have a variety of features, including:
    Three- or five-point harness
    Several harness positions to adjust as child grows
    Several-position growth buckle
    Push-button buckle
    Adjustable and removable pads
    Storage area for toys
    Converts to booster seat
    Sun shields
    Vinyl or fabric covers

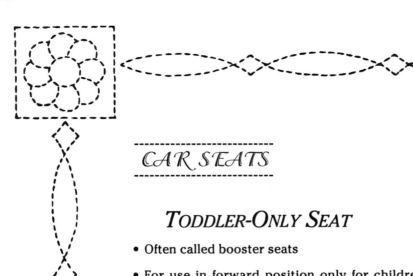

CAR SEATS

TODDLER-ONLY SEAT

- Often called booster seats
- For use in forward position only for children thirty to sixty pounds (with some exceptions)
- Vinyl or fabric covers
- To be used with car seat belts

ACCESSORIES

- Sun shade: attaches to window near baby
- Car seat cover: terry cloth, easy to remove, machine washable
- Vinyl seat protector for your car: catches food your baby drops
- Food tray: attaches to car seat
- "Doughnut pillow": a roll of fabric that holds infant's head in place
- Toys that attach to car seat to keep baby amused

Note: Be sure the car seat you buy has a label on the back that states that the car seat "meets or exceeds federal motor vehicle safety standard 213."

INFORMATION ABOUT STROLLERS AND CARRIAGES

TRADITIONAL CARRIAGES

- Primarily for infants; stay in one position

- Difficult to store and harder to maneuver

- Sturdier than most strollers

- May be quite expensive

- Lies flat for small baby to sleep in comfort

- Not as useful once baby starts sitting up

COMBINATION STROLLER/CARRIAGE

- Available from many manufacturers in a wide variety of models

- Prices range from moderate to quite expensive

- Good for both infant and young child

- Some models convert to a carriage bed

- Handles may reverse for different usages

- Removable seats and "boot" pads for washing

- Four-wheel or two-wheel braking systems

- Accessories include: basket or stroller nets, canopy, weather shield

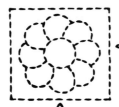

STROLLERS AND CARRIAGES

LIGHTWEIGHT STROLLERS

- Available from many manufacturers in a variety of models and price ranges
- Small, lightweight, and collapsible (some can even be folded with one hand, leaving the other free for baby, and others will stand when folded)
- Lower-priced
- Some have adjustable heights for baby's back support (sitting, sleeping, in-between)
- Easy to stow in car and carry

TWIN STROLLERS

- May be positioned face-to-face, side by side, or one behind the other
- Some can be removed to face in more than one direction
- Check weight and ease of folding

OTHER ACCESSORIES TO BE BOUGHT SEPARATELY

- Umbrella that attaches to stroller
- Toy bar that goes across the front of the stroller to keep baby amused
- Harness to snap in for very active babies
- Quilted cushion for extra padding

STROLLERS AND CARRIAGES

FEATURES TO LOOK FOR IN ANY STROLLER OR CARRIAGE

SAFETY:

- Brake locks (rear locking brake wheels)
- Strong safety belt
- Wide wheel base for stability
- Seat mounted low and deep in the frame
- Backup safety locks to prevent accidental collapse

DURABILITY:

- Rustproof
- Unbreakable pieces (nothing that can come off easily)
- Can be used as baby grows bigger

CONVENIENCE:

- Easy to use (remember: you'll be loaded down with baby and baby gear)
- Wheels that align well and make steering easy
- Handles that are the right height for you

COMFORT:

- Adequate cushioning
- Adequate sun shade
- Adjustable heights for back support

DAY OUTING CHECKLIST

- ❑ Diapers (cloth or disposable)
- ❑ Portable changing pad
- ❑ Diaper cream
- ❑ Baby wipes
- ❑ Tote bag for dirty diapers
- ❑ Cotton balls
- ❑ Baby lotion, powder, diaper rash medicine
- ❑ Change of clothes
- ❑ Towel or diaper for spills
- ❑ Toys, rattles, teething toys
- ❑ Storybooks
- ❑ Pacifier
- ❑ Bibs
- ❑ Bottles and bottle liners if needed
- ❑ Formula and can opener, juice
- ❑ Cookies, crackers, teething biscuits
- ❑ Baby food, dish, and spoon
- ❑ Hairbrush
- ❑ Baby carrier
- ❑ Stroller
- ❑ Infant seat or Sassy Seat (mealtime)
- ❑ Blanket
- ❑ Rain poncho

OVERNIGHT CHECKLIST

All items listed for everyday outings plus:

- ❑ Portable crib or its equivalent (including sheets and bumpers)
- ❑ Extra blanket
- ❑ Night light
- ❑ Extra diapers
- ❑ Pajamas
- ❑ Items baby needs to fall asleep (stuffed animal, doll)
- ❑ Clothes, including socks and undershirts
- ❑ High chair/Sassy Seat
- ❑ Extra bottles
- ❑ Bottle warmer (if used)
- ❑ Extra baby food and formula
- ❑ Shampoo and baby soap
- ❑ Detergent to wash baby's clothes
- ❑ Plastic bags for dirty diapers and clothes
- ❑ Children's acetaminophen (Tylenol or other nonaspirin brand) and thermometer
- ❑ Camera and film

AGE-APPROPRIATE TOYS

0–3 Months

Colorful room decorations

Mobiles (black-and-white ones may be easier to see)

Toys strung across crib (use only while baby cannot lift himself)

Soft dolls with clear, distinct facial features

Nonbreakable crib mirror

Music box

3 Months and Older

Soft toys baby can hold

Squeaky toys and rattles

Plastic or rubber teething toys

Gym for crib or playpen

Activity box

Bath toys

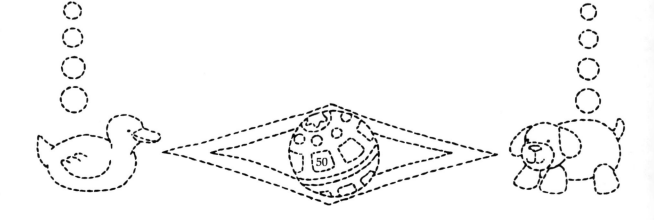

AGE-APPROPRIATE TOYS

6–12 MONTHS

Balls and rolling toys

Stacking toys

Push and pull toys

Pop-up toys

Stuffed animals

Soft cloth books or heavy cardboard books

Soft blocks

Caution: Do not give your child toys with small parts that can fit in his mouth and choke him. Check all toys for sharp edges and loose parts. Follow manufacturer's safety guidelines.

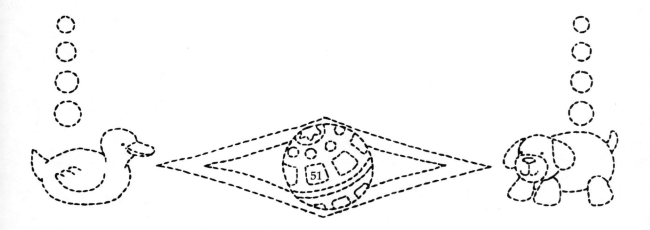

51

PART THREE

Health Maintenance

OF course, one of the most crucial (and anxiety-provoking) aspects of parenthood is taking care of baby's health. This section offers information and organizing tips that will contribute to your baby's well-being.

PEDIATRICIAN INTERVIEW FORM
Will help you evaluate doctors to determine who is best suited to your needs and personality. We suggest choosing a pediatrician before baby arrives and talking to two or three before deciding on the one you'd like to use.

FIRST AID MEDICAL SUPPLY CHART
All the necessities for routine childhood illnesses and emergency medical care.

ESSENTIAL PHONE NUMBERS
Includes doctor, fire department, police, babysitter . . . the numbers you want to be able to find FAST.

RECORD OF ALLERGIES AND REACTIONS
Many children are allergic to foods, medications, insect bites, and so forth. It's important to keep track of these reactions to have an accurate description for your doctor, and so that you can avoid the offending item in the future. Allergic reactions can grow more severe after repeated exposure to the same allergen (such as bee stings and penicillin).

INFANT/TODDLER DEVELOPMENT CHART
Broad guidelines for when to expect advances or milestones in your child's physical and mental growth; however, please remember *all children are different and develop at their own pace.*

RECORD OF BABY'S HEIGHT AND WEIGHT
Here is something else you may enjoy looking back on. It's also useful if you're concerned about your child's growth in any way.

Baby's Achievements

Gives you a place to record the developments described. You'll appreciate having this information when baby grows up.

Record of Baby's Teeth and Dental Visits

The first few teeth arrive before you know it! Keep a record of these arrivals. Then as baby becomes a toddler, record visits to the dentist and procedures done.

Schedule of Immunizations and Reactions

Although your pediatrician will notify you when your child is due for immunizations, it's useful to be aware of when they are given. This chart will also tell you what type of reactions might occur and how to treat them.

Record of Immunizations

This is an extremely important record to keep. It is imperative that babies and toddlers receive all the appropriate immunizations. In addition, you'll need this information when your child starts school and even at points during his or her adult life.

Medical/Dental Insurance Record

New babies make many visits to the doctor. It's very easy to lose track of when bills are submitted to, or reimbursed by, your insurance carrier if you don't keep an accurate record. In this case, being organized means money in your pocket!

When to Let Your Infant/Toddler Return to Day Care or Play Group

Offers some criteria for deciding when to keep your child home. This can be a tough call for a new parent.

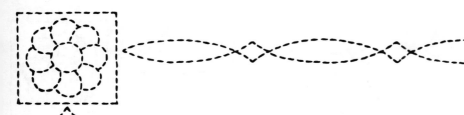

PEDIATRICIAN
INTERVIEW FORM

1. How long have you been in practice? _____

2. Where did you attend medical school? _____

3. Where did you do your pediatric residency? _____

4. Are you board-certified by the American Academy of Pediatrics?

    _____

5. Do you have a subspecialty? What is it? _____

    _____

6. Did you do any other residencies? _____

7. Do you have partners? _____

8. What are their credentials? _____

9. How much rotating is there? Will I always see you for visits? _____

    _____

10. Who covers for you when you are on vacation? _____

    _____

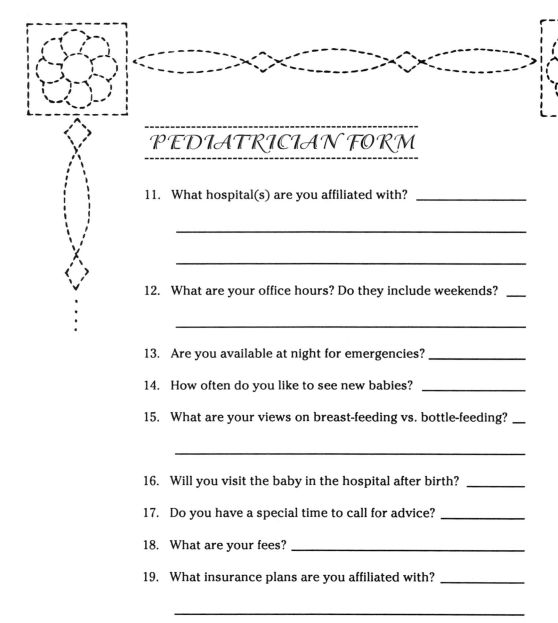

PEDIATRICIAN FORM

11. What hospital(s) are you affiliated with? _____

_____

_____

12. What are your office hours? Do they include weekends? ___

_____

13. Are you available at night for emergencies? _____

14. How often do you like to see new babies? _____

15. What are your views on breast-feeding vs. bottle-feeding? __

_____

16. Will you visit the baby in the hospital after birth? _____

17. Do you have a special time to call for advice? _____

18. What are your fees? _____

19. What insurance plans are you affiliated with? _____

_____

20. Do you have children? _____

Tip: Interview pediatricians *before* baby is born.

FIRST AID
MEDICAL SUPPLY CHART

- ❑ Nose aspirator
- ❑ Petroleum jelly
- ❑ Diaper rash cream
- ❑ Anti-sting, anti-itch lotion
- ❑ Thermometer*
- ❑ Safety scissors
- ❑ Alcohol
- ❑ Sterile gauze
- ❑ Large gauze pads
- ❑ Coldpack
- ❑ Humidifier/vaporizer
- ❑ First aid chart
- ❑ Emergency phone numbers

- ❑ Medicine spoon or dropper
- ❑ Syrup of ipecac (poison antidote)
- ❑ Tylenol/nonaspirin pain reliever
- ❑ Antibacterial cream
- ❑ Tweezers
- ❑ Sterile cotton balls
- ❑ Bottle of Pedialyte**
- ❑ Adhesive tape
- ❑ Box of assorted size Band-Aids
- ❑ Ear syringe
- ❑ Sun block
- ❑ CPR chart
- ❑ Baby wipes

* Fever strip which is placed on child's forehead or pacifier that changes color to indicate if baby has a fever may also be useful.

** Replaces electrolytes lost when child vomits or has diarrhea; Gatorade can also be used.

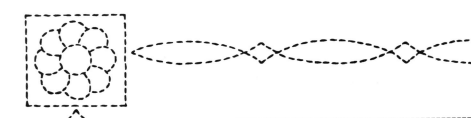 

ESSENTIAL PHONE NUMBERS

Mother at work _____

Father at work _____

Pediatrician _____
                        (name)   (number)

Hospital _____

Poison control center _____

Police/Emergency _____

Fire department _____

Dentist _____
                     (name)   (number)

Babysitter _____
                     (name   (number)

Day-care center _____
                       (name)   (number)

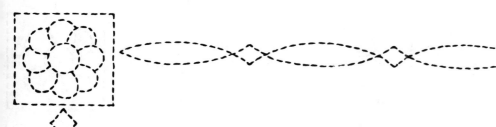

ESSENTIAL PHONE NUMBERS

Grandparents _____

                     (name)   (number)

Grandparents _____

                     (name)   (number)

Other relative _____

                     (name)   (number)

Other relative _____

                     (name)   (number)

Neighbor _____

                     (name)   (number)

Neighbor _____

                     (name)   (number)

Friend _____

                     (name)   (number)

Friend _____

                     (name)   (number)

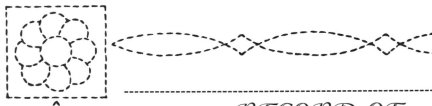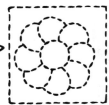

RECORD OF ALLERGIES AND REACTIONS

Use this form to record any known allergies and any possible reactions your child has experienced.

FOOD	REACTION	MEDICATION/ TREATMENT	DATE

MEDICATION	REACTION	MEDICATION/ TREATMENT	DATE

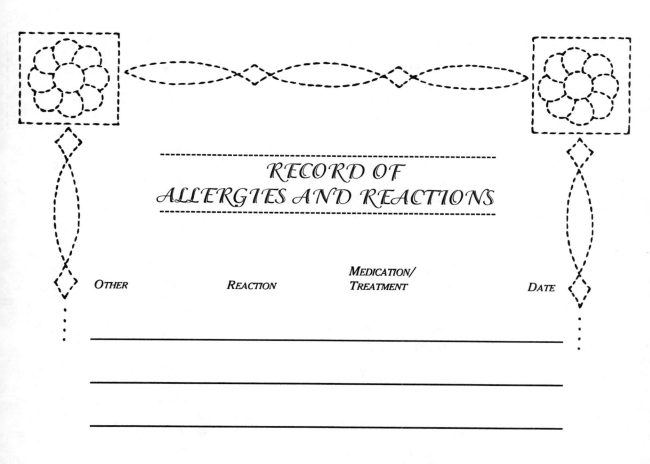

RECORD OF
ALLERGIES AND REACTIONS

OTHER	REACTION	MEDICATION/ TREATMENT	DATE

Common allergies in young children:

- Food: eggs, strawberries, milk, tomatoes, shellfish, orange juice, nuts, wheat, corn, chocolate

- Medications: antibiotics, including penicillin and sulfa

- Other: insect bites, detergents, wool, scented baby products, pollens, dust, mold

INFANT/TODDLER DEVELOPMENT CHART

The following is only a guideline. If your child does any or all of these things later than this chart suggests, this does not mean there is anything wrong with your child. Likewise, your child is not necessarily exceptional if he or she reaches these stages earlier . . . All children are different.

Begins to hold head upright
while lying on stomach ....Six weeks to three months

Notices his/her own hand ....Six weeks to three months

Smiles...Six weeks to four months

Laughs ....Two to four months

Turns self over ....Two to five months

Reaches for toy ....Three to four months

Begins whole food..........................Three to six months
(depending on your pediatrician's recommendation)

Begins cow milk ....Three to six months
(depending on your pediatrician's recommendation)

Cuts teeth...................................Three months to eighteen months

Sits unsupported...........................Five to seven months

Crawls.......................................Five to eight months

Pulls self up to stand ....Five to ten months

Says "da da" ....Six to eight months

Stands without holding on.................Seven to twelve months

Climbs up stairs ....Seven to ten months

Walks...Eight to fourteen months

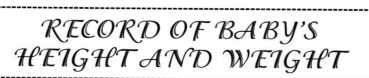

RECORD OF BABY'S HEIGHT AND WEIGHT

	HEIGHT	WEIGHT
One-month checkup		
Two-month checkup		
Three-month checkup		
Four-month checkup		
Five-month checkup		
Six-month checkup		
Seven-month checkup		
Eight-month checkup		
Nine-month checkup		
Ten-month checkup		
Eleven-month checkup		
Twelve-month checkup		
Eighteen-month checkup		
Twenty-four-month checkup		

BABY'S ACHIEVEMENTS

ACHIEVEMENT	AGE/DATE
First slept through the night	_____
First turned over	_____
First smile	_____
First laugh	_____
First played with a toy	_____
First pulled self up	_____
First sat alone	_____
First solid food	_____
First drank from a cup	_____
First crawled	_____
First step	_____
First walked across room	_____
First ice cream	_____
First cake	_____
First fed self	_____
First word	_____
First song	_____
First haircut	_____

RECORD OF BABY'S TEETH

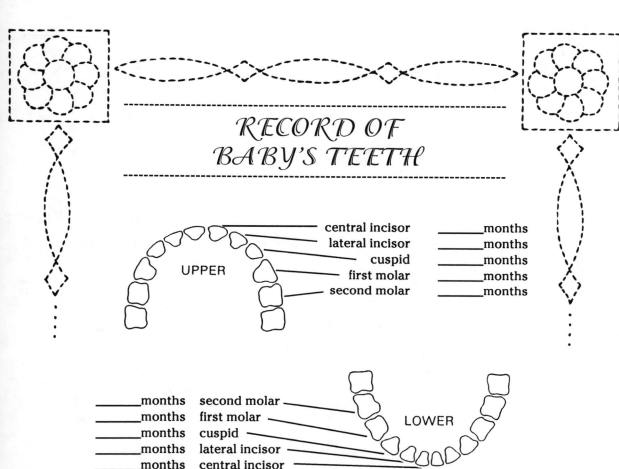

central incisor _____ months
lateral incisor _____ months
cuspid _____ months
first molar _____ months
second molar _____ months

UPPER

_____ months second molar
_____ months first molar
_____ months cuspid
_____ months lateral incisor
_____ months central incisor

LOWER

Remember:

- Never put a baby to bed with a bottle of juice or milk . . . This promotes cavities.

- Teething hurts . . . Use frozen teething rings or a teething gel on baby's gums to ease the pain.

- Take your child to the dentist for a first checkup between the ages of two and three.

- Brush your child's teeth after every meal. Rub infant's gums with soft cloth to clean.

RECORD OF
DENTAL VISITS

Dentist's Name_____Phone#_____

Address _____

DATE	CHECKUP	CLEANING	X-RAYS	FILLINGS	OTHER

Note: Children should begin seeing the dentist as soon as they have a full set of teeth.

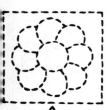

SCHEDULE OF IMMUNIZATIONS AND REACTIONS

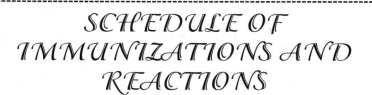

IMMUNIZATION	TIMING	REACTIONS/TREATMENT
DPT: diphtheria, pertussis (whooping cough), and tetanus	2 months	soreness at site, mild fever, irritability: treat with cold compresses, fever-reducing and pain-relieving medication

Note: In rare cases, children can have a problem with this vaccine. If your child has any history of convulsions, the doctor should be told beforehand. If your child runs a very high fever in reaction to a shot, or cries inconsolably for several hours, call your doctor.

Oral polio	2 months	no reaction
HIB (H. influenza Type B) for bacterial infections such as meningitis and pneumonia	2 months 4 months	soreness at site, mild fever: give fever-reducing, pain-relieving medication
DPT	4 months	soreness at site, mild fever
Oral polio	4 months	no reaction
DPT	6 months	mild reaction
HIB	6 months	soreness at site, fever
Oral polio	6 months	optional dosage at doctor's discretion

SCHEDULE OF IMMUNIZATIONS AND REACTIONS

IMMUNIZATION	TIMING	REACTIONS/TREATMENT
Tuberculin test	9 months/ additional at doctor's discretion	redness and mild swelling at site if positive; otherwise no reaction
Rubella (German measles), measles, mumps	15 months	mild rash, some fever: give pain-relieving, fever-reducing medication
DPT	15 months	mild reaction
Oral polio	15 months	no reaction
HIB	15 months	soreness at site, fever
DPT	4-5 years	mild reaction
Oral polio	4-5 years	no reaction
Rubella, measles, mumps	5 years (optional)	mild rash, some fever 7-10 days after shot
Tetanus and diphtheria (adult)	14-16 years	mild reaction

Note: timing of immunizations may vary slightly in accordance with individual state laws. If a child has a cold or other medical problems, immunizations may be delayed until child is well. Any unusual reactions should be reported to your pediatrician.

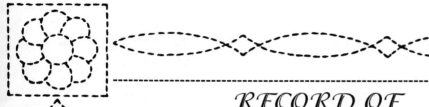
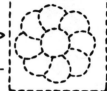

RECORD OF IMMUNIZATIONS

	DATE	*BOOSTER DATE(S)*
DPT	_____	_____
Measles	_____	_____
Mumps	_____	_____
Polio	_____	_____
HIB	_____	_____
Rubella	_____	_____
Other	_____	_____
	_____	_____
Tuberculin test	_____	_____
Blood type	_____	_____
Cholesterol test	_____	_____

NOTES: _____

_____

_____

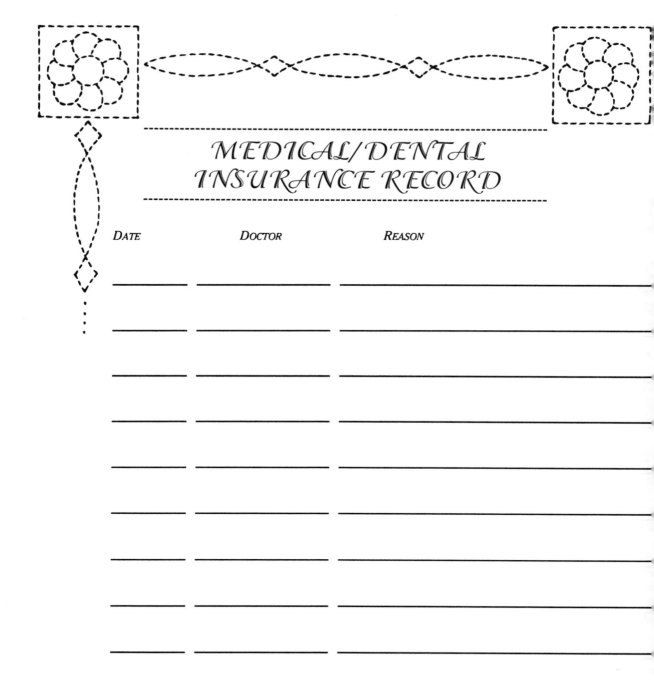

MEDICAL/DENTAL
INSURANCE RECORD

DATE *DOCTOR* *REASON*

 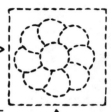

MEDICAL/DENTAL
INSURANCE RECORD

DATE SUBMITTED	INSURANCE COMPANY	DATE PAID

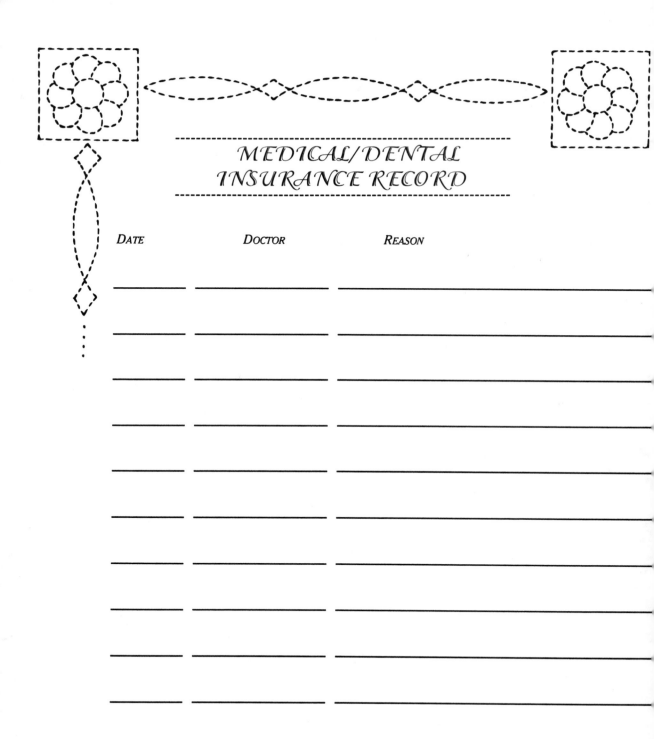

MEDICAL/DENTAL
INSURANCE RECORD

DATE	DOCTOR	REASON

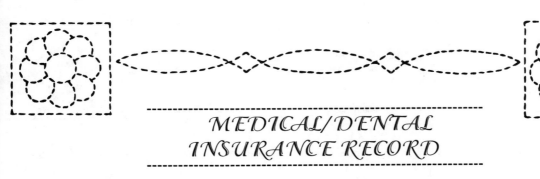

MEDICAL/DENTAL
INSURANCE RECORD

DATE SUBMITTED	INSURANCE COMPANY	DATE PAID

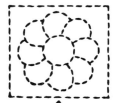

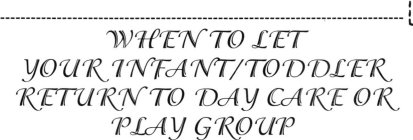

WHEN TO LET YOUR INFANT/TODDLER RETURN TO DAY CARE OR PLAY GROUP

If your child has been sick and not attending his/her day-care arrangement, when can he/she return? Here are some guidelines:

1. Temperature of 100 degrees or more (orally or rectally)—child should have normal temperature for twenty-four hours before returning.

2. Sore throat or swollen glands—child should remain at home until pediatrician says it's okay to return.

3. Red eyes or discharge from eyes—child should remain at home until pediatrician says it's okay to return.

4. Croupy, hacking, or persistent cough—child should remain home until cough subsides.

5. Diarrhea or vomiting—child should remain home until well for twenty-four hours.

6. Sores or rash on body or face—child should remain home until cleared by pediatrician.

7. Yellow or green nasal discharge—child should remain home until symptom clears.

Note: These guidelines apply to toddlers and older children. When infants are ill, check with your pediatrician.

These guidelines are courtesy of Stephen Boris, M.D., F.A.A.P., Mamaroneck, New York.

PART FOUR

Feeding

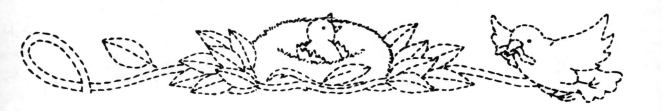

FEEDING a new baby is always of great concern to parents who wonder when to feed, how much to feed, when to start solid food, when to start giving cow's milk, and so on. We won't try to tell you when to do these things because these decisions should be made with the help of your pediatrician. What we will do in this section is provide you with useful charts for recording all those important aspects of feeding your baby—and yourself.

FEEDING TRACKING FORMS
If you're bottle-feeding, you'll want to keep track of how much milk baby is taking and how often. If you're breast-feeding, you'll want to note how often baby is nursing and for how long. It will help you to begin establishing a schedule and may be useful information for your pediatrician if baby is not gaining enough weight.

FOOD INTRODUCTION RECORD
It is highly recommended that you give a baby only one new food every five days in order to determine which food may trigger an allergic reaction. After a few weeks it can be hard to remember which foods were introduced when. This form will serve as a reminder.

INFORMATION ABOUT FORMULA
Formula comes in so many different varieties. We've provided you with a chart to show all types available. You can decide which formula is best for you.

INFORMATION ABOUT BABY BOTTLES AND NIPPLES
Here's some basic information you'll need when selecting these items.

MOTHER'S DIET/CALORIE RECORD

Most of us put on a few unwanted pounds during pregnancy and may have to do some dieting. (Don't cut back too much if you're nursing—you'll need the extra calories for baby.) Mother deserves a record of her own, too, so here's one to note your calories and exchanges so you can get back in shape.

MOTHER'S EXERCISE RECORD

Try a little exercise to shed those extra pounds more quickly and strengthen those stomach muscles. Every little bit helps— even if you can only do a few minutes at a time, write it down and see how the minutes add up.

HOMEMADE BABY FOOD
BABY FOOD RECIPES

Although commercial baby foods are greatly improved these days (less salt, sugar, and preservatives), many new parents still prefer to make their own baby food. If you find some good recipes, here's the place to store them.

GROCERY LIST

When you have to buy so many items for baby in addition to your regular groceries, you almost always forget something. These lists are foolproof—take them with you whenever you go shopping.

BOTTLE-FEEDING TRACKING FORM

If you are bottle-feeding, fill in the time feeding began and the total number of ounces drunk. Your new baby will probably need to be fed every four hours. Keep these records until you feel comfortable that your baby is drinking enough and gaining weight.

MONDAY

Time started   _____   _____   _____   _____   _____   _____   _____   _____

Amount (ounces)   _____   _____   _____   _____   _____   _____   _____   _____

TUESDAY

Time started   _____   _____   _____   _____   _____   _____   _____   _____

Amount (ounces)   _____   _____   _____   _____   _____   _____   _____   _____

WEDNESDAY

Time started   _____   _____   _____   _____   _____   _____   _____   _____

Amount (ounces)   _____   _____   _____   _____   _____   _____   _____   _____

BOTTLE-FEEDING TRACKING FORM

THURSDAY

Time started   ____ ____ ____ ____ ____ ____ ____ ____

Amount (ounces)   ____ ____ ____ ____ ____ ____ ____ ____

FRIDAY

Time started   ____ ____ ____ ____ ____ ____ ____ ____

Amount (ounces)   ____ ____ ____ ____ ____ ____ ____ ____

SATURDAY

Time started   ____ ____ ____ ____ ____ ____ ____ ____

Amount (ounces)   ____ ____ ____ ____ ____ ____ ____ ____

SUNDAY

Time started   ____ ____ ____ ____ ____ ____ ____ ____

Amount (ounces)   ____ ____ ____ ____ ____ ____ ____ ____

82

BREAST-FEEDING TRACKING FORM

If you are breast-feeding, fill in the time nursing began and ended. Remember to alternate breasts and note which breast you ended with so that you begin with the same one next time. Your new baby will probably need to be fed more often than every four hours since it is difficult to determine how much milk the baby's receiving. Keep these records until you feel comfortable that your baby is drinking enough and gaining weight.

MONDAY

Time started _____ _____ _____ _____ _____ _____ _____ _____

Time ended _____ _____ _____ _____ _____ _____ _____ _____

TUESDAY

Time started _____ _____ _____ _____ _____ _____ _____ _____

Time ended _____ _____ _____ _____ _____ _____ _____ _____

WEDNESDAY

Time started _____ _____ _____ _____ _____ _____ _____ _____

Time ended _____ _____ _____ _____ _____ _____ _____ _____

BREAST-FEEDING TRACKING FORM

THURSDAY

Time started   _____ _____ _____ _____ _____ _____ _____ _____

Time ended   _____ _____ _____ _____ _____ _____ _____ _____

FRIDAY

Time started   _____ _____ _____ _____ _____ _____ _____ _____

Time ended   _____ _____ _____ _____ _____ _____ _____ _____

SATURDAY

Time started   _____ _____ _____ _____ _____ _____ _____ _____

Time ended   _____ _____ _____ _____ _____ _____ _____ _____

SUNDAY

Time started   _____ _____ _____ _____ _____ _____ _____ _____

Time ended   _____ _____ _____ _____ _____ _____ _____ _____

FOOD INTRODUCTION RECORD

The first solid food babies are usually given is rice cereal. Then they are gradually introduced to other cereals. Next, most pediatricians recommend fruits, followed by vegetables and meats. Be sure to heed your doctor's suggestions. Some babies are allergic to or cannot tolerate certain foods, so it is a good idea to introduce one new food at a time and to wait five days before trying another new food.

Foods that most often cause allergic reactions are: nuts, shellfish, chocolate, wheat, orange juice, berries, tomatoes, eggs, milk, and corn.

Do not give your baby honey for the first year and a half because it may cause botulism.

FOOD	AMOUNT	DATE	REACTIONS

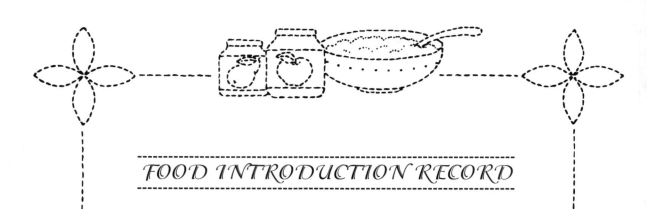

FOOD INTRODUCTION RECORD

FOOD	AMOUNT	DATE	REACTIONS
____	____	____	____
____	____	____	____
____	____	____	____
____	____	____	____
____	____	____	____
____	____	____	____
____	____	____	____
____	____	____	____
____	____	____	____
____	____	____	____

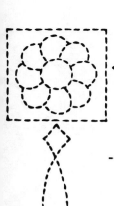

INFORMATION ABOUT FORMULA

Ask your pediatrician what brand of formula you should give your baby. Most formulas are milk-based. Babies with allergies or digestive problems may fare better with soy-based or other formulas.

Most prepared formulas come in the following forms:

1. Ready-to-use (no dilution necessary)

   - 32-ounce can

   - 8-ounce can

   - Disposable bottles; 4 ounces, 6 ounces, and 8 ounces

2. Concentrated (must be diluted with water)

   - 13-ounce can

3. Powdered (must be mixed with water)

   - 16-ounce can

4. Soy formulas

   - For babies who have trouble digesting regular formula. (Your doctor will tell you if your baby needs this type.)

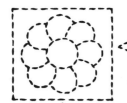

FORMULA

5. "Advanced formulas"

- Intended for use by older babies. By the time most babies would need this formula, they are usually ready for cow's milk.

Ready-to-use formulas are more expensive but more convenient. If you decide to use the concentrated or powdered forms, be sure to follow diluting and mixing instructions carefully so baby gets the right amount of nutrients.

Tips on storage: Formula in original bottles and cans does not need to be refrigerated. If you open a can and divide it into individual bottles, you must refrigerate the bottles. If you don't use all of it in 24 hours, then throw it out. Some people prefer not to prepare all the bottles at one time. You may simply cover the open can with aluminum foil and store it in the refrigerator. Mark the can with the date and time opened so you know to discard it after 24 hours.

Tips on storage of breast milk: Breast milk may be stored in the refrigerator for 24-48 hours. Breast milk may also be frozen for up to two weeks. Purchase special bottles for this purpose or sterile plastic containers since glass might crack.

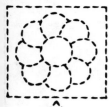

INFORMATION ABOUT BABY BOTTLES AND NIPPLES

Glass, plastic, and disposable bottles are available in four-ounce (for the younger infant) and eight-ounce sizes. All can be covered with caps to protect from spillage and dirt.

GLASS BOTTLES

—Heavy to hold.

—May break or chip if dropped.

—Very durable if you plan to sterilize your bottles (see section on cleaning below).

PLASTIC BOTTLES

—Light in weight and easy to hold.

—Available in clear plastic as well as opaque colors; may be decorated with pretty designs.

—Different manufacturers produce bottles in various shapes. Some are easier for baby to hold, such as those with indentations or a hole in the middle, or handles that allow baby's fingers to grip the bottle. Traditional (round) bottles, however, are easier to clean than the more unusually shaped ones.

DISPOSABLE BOTTLES

—Consist of a hard plastic holder in which a soft plastic bottle-shaped bag is inserted. As baby drinks, the bag deflates. This results in less air in the bottle and less air for baby to swallow. After feeding, the plastic bag insert is discarded.

—Eliminates bottle washing.

—More expensive than other bottles.

—Possibility of leakage, if bag is not inserted properly.

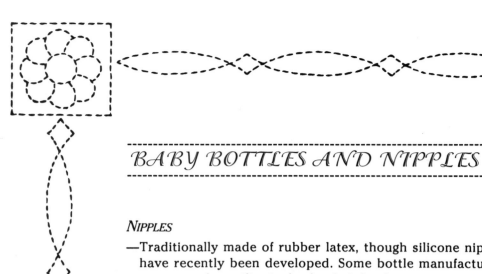

BABY BOTTLES AND NIPPLES

NIPPLES

—Traditionally made of rubber latex, though silicone nipples have recently been developed. Some bottle manufacturers recommend specific nipples for their bottles.

—Come in a variety of shapes. Some are round, some are square, and some try to replicate a mother's nipple shape. Your child may prefer one shape over another.

—For premature or small infants whose sucking ability is weak, softer nipples are available.

—There are nipples that work best with formula, milk, juice, or water. Each has a different hole or opening to allow optimal flow of liquid. The manufacturer's packaging clearly notes which kind of nipple you are buying.

CLEANING BOTTLES

Many doctors no longer feel sterilizing of bottles is necessary. Check with your pediatrician. Washing with warm, soapy water may be sufficient. Electric and stove-top sterilizers are available, as are special dishwasher racks to hold bottles and nipples. If you cannot find them in a store, contact your dishwasher manufacturer. Nipple brushes and bottle brushes are a must for washing by hand.

BOTTLE WARMERS

Warming the formula is not necessary, but some babies prefer it warm. Electric models are now available. Never heat a baby bottle in a microwave oven.

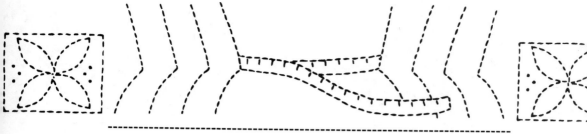

MOTHER'S
DIET/CALORIE RECORD

STARTING WEIGHT _____ GOAL WEIGHT _____

Calories/exchanges allowed _____ Amount used _____

Breakfast		*Calories/exchanges*
Protein	_____	_____
Dairy	_____	_____
Fruit	_____	_____
Vegetables	_____	_____
Bread/cereal	_____	_____
Fat	_____	_____
Other	_____	_____

Lunch		*Calories/exchanges*
Protein	_____	_____
Dairy	_____	_____
Fruit	_____	_____
Vegetables	_____	_____

MOTHER'S DIET/CALORIE RECORD

Lunch   *Calories/exchanges*

Bread/cereal _____   _____

Fat   _____   _____

Other   _____   _____

Dinner   *Calories/exchanges*

Protein   _____   _____

Dairy   _____   _____

Fruit   _____   _____

Vegetables   _____   _____

Bread/cereal _____   _____

Fat   _____   _____

Other   _____   _____

Snack   _____   _____

TOTAL FOR DAY   _____

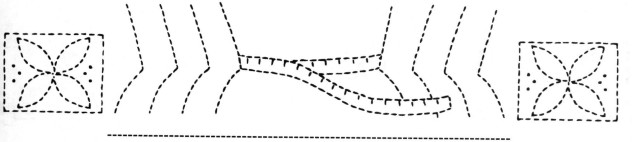

MOTHER'S
EXERCISE RECORD

Try to do a little bit of exercise every day. Even if it's just a few minutes at a time. You'll feel better physically and emotionally, and regain your shape faster. (See mail-order section for exercise videos.)

DATE	TYPE OF EXERCISE	DURATION (MINUTES)

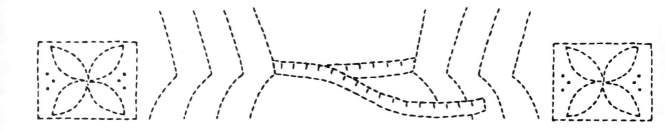

MOTHER'S EXERCISE RECORD

DATE	TYPE OF EXERCISE	DURATION (MINUTES)

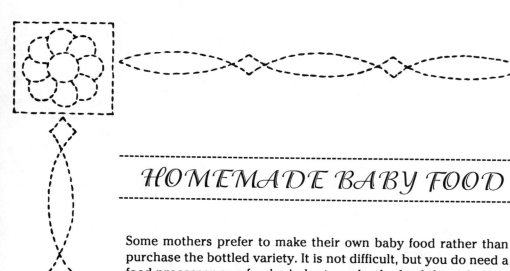

HOMEMADE BABY FOOD

Some mothers prefer to make their own baby food rather than purchase the bottled variety. It is not difficult, but you do need a food processor or a food grinder to make the food the right consistency.

To make sure that your child gets the right amount of nutrition from the food you make, we recommend that you consult some recipe books for ideas. Here are some suggestions:

The Baby Cookbook, by Karen Knight and Jeannie Lumley
The Vegetarian Mother Baby Book, by Rose Elliot
Instant Baby Food, by Linda McDonald
Feed Me! I'm Yours, by Vicki Lansky
The Natural Baby Food Cookbook, by Margaret Elizabeth Kenda and Phyllis S. Williams
The Complete New Guide to Preparing Baby Foods, by Sue Castle
Baby Food Cookbooks & Recipe References: An Index, by the Cookbook Consortium Information Division Staff, ed.
Into the Mouths of Babes: A Natural Foods Cookbook for Infants & Toddlers, by Susan Firkaly

Handy Tip: Make batches of food and freeze in ice trays. Thaw one cube at a time to make one serving for baby.

BABY FOOD RECIPES

NAME OF DISH_____ Yield_____

Ingredients:

Directions:

NAME OF DISH_____ Yield_____

Ingredients:

Directions:

BABY FOOD RECIPES

NAME OF DISH_____ Yield_____

Ingredients:

Directions:

NAME OF DISH_____ Yield_____

Ingredients:

Directions:

GROCERY LIST

CLEANING PRODUCTS
_____
_____
_____
_____

DAIRY
_____
_____
_____
_____

CANNED GOODS
_____
_____
_____
_____

PAPER GOODS
_____
_____
_____
_____

MEAT/POULTRY/FISH
_____
_____
_____
_____

FRUIT/VEGETABLES
_____
_____
_____
_____

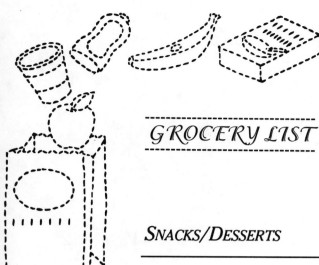

GROCERY LIST

SNACKS/DESSERTS
_____
_____
_____
_____

BREAD/CRACKERS
_____
_____
_____
_____

PASTA/RICE/GRAINS
_____
_____
_____
_____

CONDIMENTS
_____
_____
_____
_____

FROZEN FOODS
_____
_____
_____
_____

BEVERAGES
_____
_____
_____
_____

GROCERY LIST

BABY FOOD—CEREAL

_____

_____

_____

_____

BABY FOOD—COOKIES

_____

_____

_____

_____

BABY FOOD—MEAT

_____

_____

_____

_____

BABY FOOD—VEGETABLES

_____

_____

_____

_____

BABY FOOD—FRUIT/JUICE

_____

_____

_____

_____

MISCELLANEOUS

_____

_____

_____

_____

GROCERY LIST

- ☐ Formula
- ☐ Cotton balls
- ☐ Baby shampoo
- ☐ Diapers
- ☐ A&D ointment/Vaseline
- ☐ Sunscreen
- ☐ Teething toys
- ☐ Pedialyte
- ☐ Baby wipes

- ☐ Bottle liners
- ☐ Baby soap
- ☐ Baby powder
- ☐ Q-tips
- ☐ Baby Tylenol
- ☐ Teething gel
- ☐ Prescriptions
- ☐ Disposable bibs
- ☐ Diaper liners

Household toiletries:

_____

_____

_____

_____

PART FIVE

Selecting and Evaluating Child Care

CHOOSING a care giver or a day-care center for your child can be a very emotional issue. You'll feel better about it if you are prepared and practical about deciding who to entrust with the care of your child. The interview/evaluation forms we've included in this section are for three different situations.

ADULT CARE GIVER INTERVIEW FORM

The types of questions you will want to ask someone who regularly takes care of your child will differ somewhat from those asked of an occasional babysitter. Please add your own questions to the interview form.

TEENAGE BABYSITTER INTERVIEW FORM

A little shorter than the previous form. While you are concerned for your child's welfare, you are not making a decision as to whether someone can nurture your child on an ongoing basis. But you do want someone trustworthy, reliable, and mature enough to handle an emergency. Here are some questions to determine that.

DAY-CARE/PRESCHOOL EVALUATION FORM

Another tough decision. There are big differences among day-care centers; again, use our form as a guide and add your own questions.

BABYSITTER INSTRUCTION SHEET

Allows you to leave all the information you need in one convenient place.

BABYSITTER DIRECTORY

Provides a handy place to keep a list of babysitters and relevant information about them,

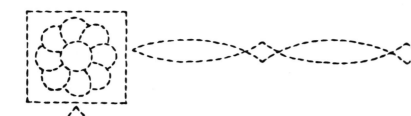

ADULT CARE GIVER INTERVIEW FORM

Applicant's name _____

Address _____

Phone number _____

1. What experience do you have with caring for children? _____

   _____

2. What was your last job? _____

   How long were you there?_____

3. If child care, what were your exact duties? Please describe what you did on a typical day._____

   _____

4. Can you provide references? _____

   _____

   _____

5. What do you think your former employer will say about you?_____

   _____

6. Why are you no longer working there? _____

   _____

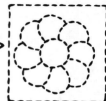

ADULT CARE GIVER INTERVIEW FORM

7. If previous job was not child care, why have you decided to work in child care? _____

8. Have you ever taken a babysitter or child CPR course? _____

   Where was it given? _____

   When? _____

9. What was the level of school you attended? _____

10. Do you smoke? _____

11. Do you have any health problems? _____

12. Are you a U.S. citizen or do you have a green card? _____

   _____

13. Do you have a driver's license? _____

   Car? _____

14. Can you stay late if I have to work late or go out of town? _____

   _____

15. Where do you live? _____

   Can you get here by _____A.M. so that I can get to work on time?

   _____

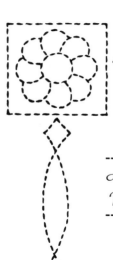

ADULT CARE GIVER INTERVIEW FORM

16. Describe all aspects of job and discuss these with the applicant. Be certain to stress your philosophy and those things that are most important to you, including:

   • Hours of duty

   • Job requirements—feeding, bathing, taking child for walks, taking child to play with other children

   • Household responsibilities—laundry, cleaning, cooking

17. Be specific about how much you wish the care giver to be a part of the family. For example, will she eat meals with the family, spend leisure time with the family, etc.

18. If care giver is to be live-in:

   • Show her the bedroom and bathroom she would use

   • Be specific about what hours she is expected to be on duty

   • Establish whether she goes home on weekends or lives with you seven days a week

   • Discuss days off

   • Explain how you feel about her entertaining friends

19. Discuss salary and any benefits you might provide, including paid vacations.

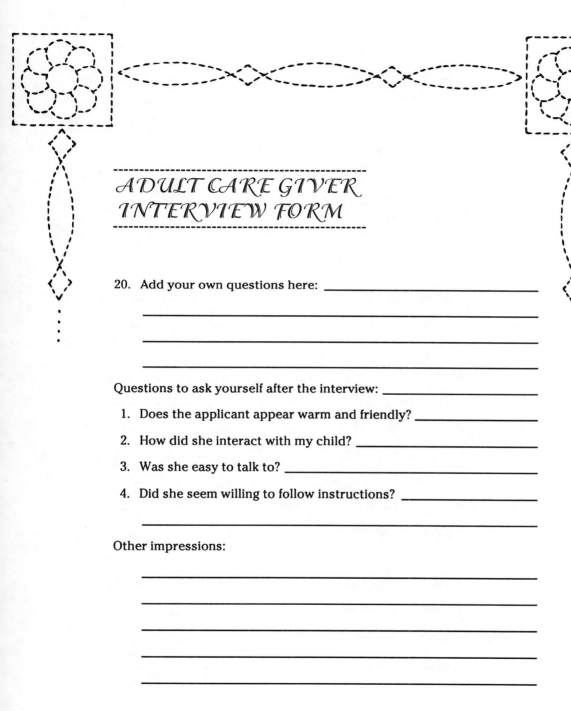

ADULT CARE GIVER INTERVIEW FORM

20. Add your own questions here: _____

_____

_____

_____

Questions to ask yourself after the interview: _____

1. Does the applicant appear warm and friendly? _____

2. How did she interact with my child? _____

3. Was she easy to talk to? _____

4. Did she seem willing to follow instructions? _____

_____

Other impressions:

_____

_____

_____

_____

_____

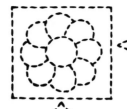

TEENAGE BABYSITTER INTERVIEW FORM

Applicant's name _____ Phone number _____

Address _____

_____

1. How old are you? _____

2. Have you ever babysat before? _____

3. Can you give references? _____

_____

4. Do you have any brothers or sisters? _____

5. Have you ever babysat an infant before? _____

6. Have you ever fed an infant? _____

7. Have you ever changed an infant's diapers? _____

8. Have you ever taken a babysitter course or a child CPR course? ___

   When and where was it given? _____

9. Which days/nights are you available? _____

_____

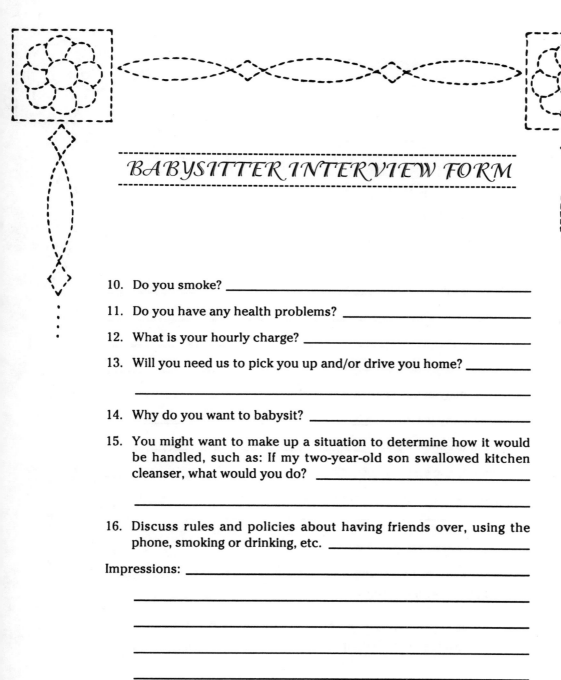

BABYSITTER INTERVIEW FORM

10. Do you smoke? _____

11. Do you have any health problems? _____

12. What is your hourly charge? _____

13. Will you need us to pick you up and/or drive you home? _____

    _____

14. Why do you want to babysit? _____

15. You might want to make up a situation to determine how it would be handled, such as: If my two-year-old son swallowed kitchen cleanser, what would you do? _____

    _____

16. Discuss rules and policies about having friends over, using the phone, smoking or drinking, etc. _____

Impressions: _____

_____

_____

_____

_____

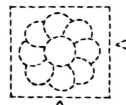

DAY-CARE CENTER OR PRESCHOOL EVALUATION FORM

Name of center or school _____

Address _____

Telephone _____

1. What are the hours the center/school is open? _____

2. How many children are in the center/school? _____

    How many per room? _____

    What are their ages? _____

    What is the staff/child ratio? _____

3. What are the qualifications and credentials of the director and staff? _____

    _____

    _____

4. What is the philosophy of the school or center? _____

    _____

5. Is there any parent participation? _____

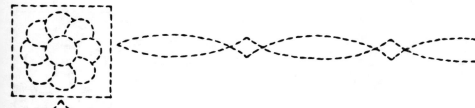

DAY-CARE/PRESCHOOL EVALUATION FORM

6. How are parents notified when there is a problem? _____

_____

7. Is there a religious affiliation? _____

8. What kind of license or accreditation does the center/school have?

_____

9. How long has the center/school been in business? _____

10. What is the cost? _____

_____

Does it increase as the child gets older? _____

11. Is transportation available? _____

What does it cost? _____

12. Describe a typical day? _____

_____

13. Do children go outside during the day? _____

14. What is the policy for sick children? _____

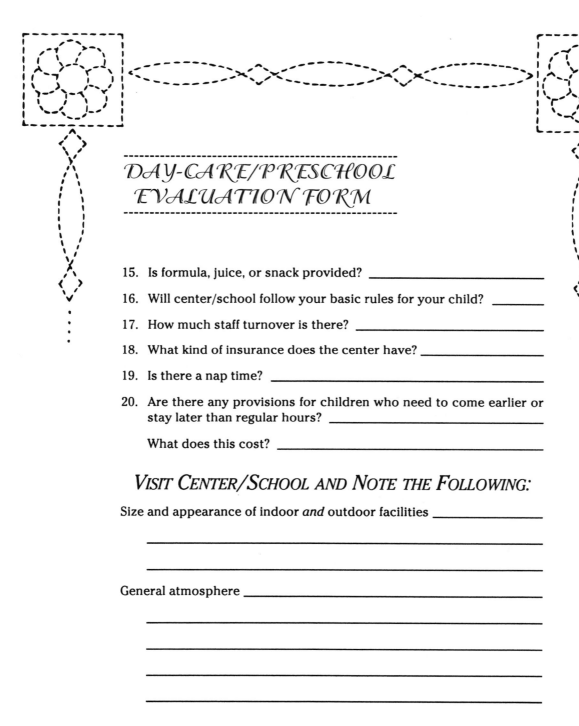

DAY-CARE/PRESCHOOL EVALUATION FORM

15. Is formula, juice, or snack provided? _____

16. Will center/school follow your basic rules for your child? _____

17. How much staff turnover is there? _____

18. What kind of insurance does the center have? _____

19. Is there a nap time? _____

20. Are there any provisions for children who need to come earlier or stay later than regular hours? _____

    What does this cost? _____

VISIT CENTER/SCHOOL AND NOTE THE FOLLOWING:

Size and appearance of indoor *and* outdoor facilities _____

_____

_____

General atmosphere _____

_____

_____

_____

_____

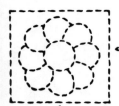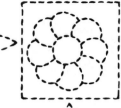

DAY-CARE/PRESCHOOL EVALUATION FORM

Do children look happy? _____

Are children busy? _____

Is the staff interested and involved? _____

How are the children disciplined? _____

_____

Is there a rest/nap area? _____

Is there an eating area? Is it clean? _____

How clean is the entire facility, toys, equipment, etc.? _____

Are there enough toys/activities? _____

Are there sick children present? _____

Is there a comfortable transition from one activity to another? _____

_____

Do the children have their own cubbyholes? _____

_____

_____

_____

_____

BABYSITTER
INSTRUCTION SHEET

Our name _____

Address _____

_____

Our phone number _____

Child(ren) name(s) _____

and ages(s) _____

We are at: _____

Name/address _____

_____

Phone number _____

Emergency phone numbers

Police _____Fire _____

Ambulance _____Poison center _____

Neighbor _____

Relative _____

116

INSTRUCTION SHEET

Instructions for today:

Meals & snacks _____

Bedtime _____

Medications _____

❏   Change diaper every _____ hours

❏   Change diaper before bed

❏   Give bath

TV instructions _____

Other instructions _____

IMPORTANT: Never leave child alone

Take child out of house if fire is suspected

Call fire department from next door

Don't open the door for anyone

PARENTS REMEMBER TO: Show babysitter how doors and
locks open
Show locations of exits
Show locations of alarms or smoke
detectors

117

BABYSITTER DIRECTORY

Name_____ Phone_____ Age_____

Address_____

_____

Times available_____

Hourly wage_____ Needs transportation_____

Comments_____

_____

Name_____ Phone_____ Age_____

Address_____

_____

Times available_____

Hourly wage_____ Needs transportation_____

Comments_____

_____

BABYSITTER DIRECTORY

Name_____ Phone_____ Age_____

Address_____

_____

Times available_____

Hourly wage_____ Needs transportation_____

Comments_____

_____

Name_____ Phone_____ Age_____

Address_____

_____

Times available_____

Hourly wage_____ Needs transportation_____

Comments_____

_____

BABYSITTER DIRECTORY

Name_____ Phone_____ Age_____

Address_____

_____

Times available_____

Hourly wage_____ Needs transportation_____

Comments_____

_____

Name_____ Phone_____ Age_____

Address_____

_____

Times available_____

Hourly wage_____ Needs transportation_____

Comments_____

_____

PART SIX

Buying by Mail Order

THERE are many, many places to shop for children's products today—no doubt your friends will have some great recommendations for you. But if your time for shopping is limited, and you don't want to carry heavy packages while you're pregnant or busy with baby, we'd like to suggest that you consider mail order.

There are literally hundreds of mail-order companies selling the following: maternity clothes, children's clothing, equipment and furniture, toys, books, records, tapes, linens, birth announcements, and many other items useful for babies. Included in this section you will find:

TIPS FOR BUYING BY MAIL ORDER

If you haven't done much ordering by mail, these suggestions may be helpful to you.

MAIL-ORDER PURCHASING RECORD

Here's the place to keep a record of items ordered.

MAIL-ORDER RESOURCES

This is by no means a complete list of all mail-order companies offering child-related products. However, most of the better-known ones are represented here, and there should be enough choices to allow you to purchase almost anything you might need by mail. Companies are listed by the type of product they sell.

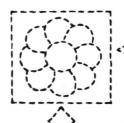

TIPS FOR BUYING BY MAIL ORDER

1. Always keep track of what you have ordered, when you ordered, and your method of payment.

2. Use 800 numbers and credit cards to speed your order.

3. Never send cash.

4. Read size information carefully. If you're still not sure, call the company or catalog and ask about how sizes run.

5. Don't be afraid to return. Always save all packing materials until you are sure you will not be returning anything.

6. Don't be afraid to use the customer service number most mail-order companies provide if you want to check on your order or a return.

7. Remember colors may not look exactly the same as they appear in the catalog.

8. Allow three to six weeks for delivery of your order.

9. Credits take two billing cycles to appear on your credit card statement, so don't panic if you don't see them right away.

10. If you have trouble with a mail-order company, contact the Federal Trade Commission, the post office, your state attorney general's office, and/or the Direct Marketing Association (6 East Forty-Third Street, New York, NY 10017) for help.

11. By law, if a mail-order company cannot ship to you in 30 days of receipt of your order (unless otherwise stated in their offer), the company must give you the option of receiving a refund or waiting for the order to be filled.

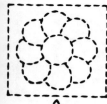

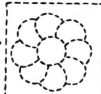

MAIL-ORDER PURCHASING RECORD

Company/catalog ordered from (include address & phone)

_____

_____

Items ordered:

_____

_____

_____

Date ordered_____Method of payment _____

Received ❑   Returned ❑   Date_____   Refund received ❑

Company/catalog ordered from (include address & phone)

_____

_____

Items ordered:

_____

_____

_____

Date ordered_____Method of payment _____

Received ❑   Returned ❑   Date_____   Refund received ❑

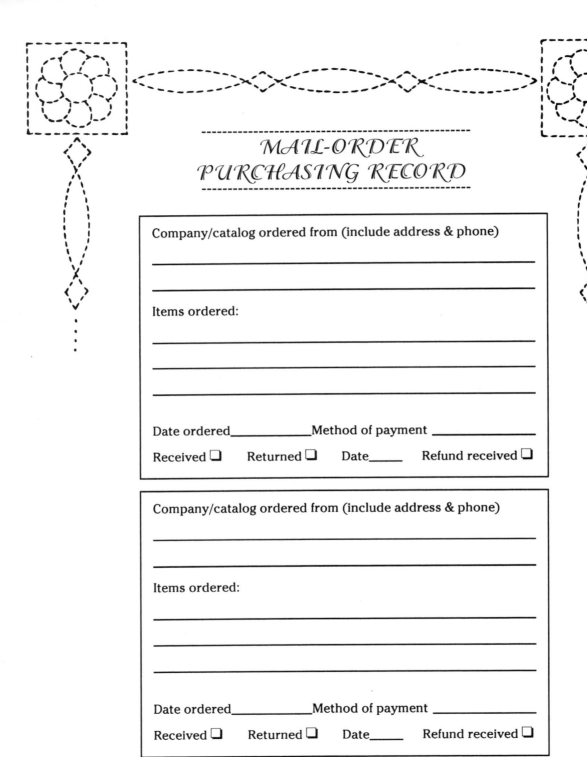

MAIL-ORDER PURCHASING RECORD

Company/catalog ordered from (include address & phone)

_____

_____

Items ordered:

_____

_____

_____

Date ordered_____Method of payment _____

Received ❑   Returned ❑   Date_____   Refund received ❑

Company/catalog ordered from (include address & phone)

_____

_____

Items ordered:

_____

_____

_____

Date ordered_____Method of payment _____

Received ❑   Returned ❑   Date_____   Refund received ❑

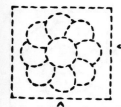

MAIL-ORDER RESOURCES

Baby Announcements

A STAR IS BORN
6462 Montgomery Avenue
Van Nuys, CA 91406
(818) 785-5656

Looks like the slates used to start the "take"of a movie.

BABYGRAM
201 Main Street
Suite 600
Fort Worth, TX 76102
(800) 345-BABY

Looks like a real Mailgram, with your message and baby's photo. Can obtain envelopes to address in advance.

BABY NAME-A-GRAMS
Box 8465
Saint Louis, MO 63132
(314) 966-BABY

Baby's name is drawn in calligraphy to become a design such as a sheep or a bear.

CRADLEGRAM
Box 16-4135
Miami, FL 33116
(305) 595-6050

Printed on pink or blue paper; name and vital statistics put into rhyming message.

HEART THOUGHTS INC.
6200 East Central, Suite 100
Wichita, KS 67208
(316) 688-5781

Formal, with baby's own calling card. Can be ordered in advance and card inserted when baby is born.

H & F PRODUCTS
3734 West Ninety-fifth Street
Leawood, KS 66206
(800) 338-4001

Many designs with matching thank you notes. Envelopes available in advance.

BIRTHWRITES
Box 684
Owings Mill, MD 21117
(301) 363-0872

Offers a wide variety.

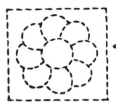

Baby Equipment

BABY BUNZ & CO.
Box 1717
Sebastopol, CA 95473
(707) 829-5347
Sells cloth diapers and diaper covers.

BABY'S COMFORT PRODUCTS
1740 North Old Pueblo Drive
Tucson, AZ 87545
(602) 624-1892
Car seat covers and other useful items

BABY & COMPANY
Box 906
New Monmouth, NJ 07748
(908) 671-7777
Supplies for infants and toddlers.

BEST SELECTION INC.
2626 Live Oak Highway
Yuba City, CA 95991
(916) 673-9798
Useful baby equipment and safety items.

BIRTH AND BEGINNINGS
6828 Route 128
Laytonsville Shopping Center
Laytonsville, MD 20879
(301) 990-7925
Diaper covers, training pants, and other items.

CHASELLE, INC.
9645 Gerwig Lane
Columbia, MD 21046
(800) CHASELLE;
(800) 492-7840 in MD
Baby supplies that are also sold to day-care centers.

COMPARE AND SAVE PREMIUM CATALOG
Box 88828
Seattle, WA 98188
(800) COMPARE
Discounted baby merchandise from diapers to high chairs.

DESIGNER DIAPERS
3800 Wendell Drive
Suite 403
Atlanta, GA 30336
(800) 541-7604;
(404) 691-4403
Disposable diapers. Expensive but cute gift item.

GOOD GEAR FOR LITTLE PEOPLE
Washington, ME 04574
(207) 845-2211
Good selection of carriers, outerwear, and other items for children at reasonable prices.

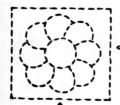

BABY EQUIPMENT

HAND-IN-HAND
9180 Le Saint Drive
Fairfield, OH 45014
(800) 543-4343
Lots of useful equipment for infants and toddlers.

HEIR AFFAIR
625 Russell Drive
Meridien, MS 39301
(800) 332-4347; (601) 484-4323
Baby equipment and toys.

MOTHER'S NETWORK
875 Avenue of the Americas
Suite 2001
New York, NY 10001
(212) 239-0510
Excellent catalog full of useful items.

ONE STEP AHEAD
Box 46
Deerfield, IL 60015
(800) 274-8440
Nice selection of baby and toddler supplies.

PERFECTLY SAFE
7425 Whipple Avenue NW
North Canton, OH 44720
(216) 494-4366
Safety and other useful items for infants, toddlers, small children, moderately priced.

SELFCARE CATALOG
Box 130
Mandeville, LA 70470
(800) 345-3371
Health and safety items for babies and children.

SENSATIONAL BEGINNINGS
Box 2009
430 North Monroe
Monroe, MI 48161
(800) 444-2147;
(313) 242-2147
Good selection of infant and toddler equipment.

SEVENTH GENERATION
Colchester, VT 05446
(800) 456-1177
Environmentally safe disposable diapers, cloth diaper covers, cotton flannel diapers, chlorine-free baby wipes, "unpetroleum" jelly for baby.

THE CHILDREN'S WAREHOUSE
1110 Technology Place
Suite 108
West Palm Beach, FL 33407
(no phone orders)
Basic baby equipment from name-brand manufacturers. Some items at sale prices.

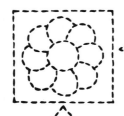

BABY EQUIPMENT

THE RIGHT START
Right Start Plaza
5334 Sterling Center Drive
Westlake Village, CA 91361
(800) LITTLE 1
Safety and other useful items
for infants, toddlers, and small
children.

The following manufacturer's will send you catalogs but do not sell by mail order:

APRICA KASSAI USA INC
Box 25408
Anaheim, CA 92825
(800) 444-3312;
(714) 634-0402
Will send catalog on strollers,
but you must buy in retail
stores.

CENTURY PRODUCTS INC.
9600 Valley View Road
Macedonia, OH 44056
(216) 468-2000
Will send literature on their
strollers and other baby equipment.

**GRACO CHILDREN'S
PRODUCTS INC.**
Route 23
Elverson, PA 19520
(800) 345-4109;
(215) 286-5921
Will send literature on strollers
and other baby equipment. For
purchase only in retail stores.

PEREGO U.S.A. INC.
3625 Independent Drive
Ft. Wayne, IN 46818
(219) 482-8191
Will send literature on their
strollers; not sold by mail.

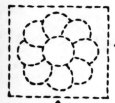

Books and Cassettes on Parenting

BABY SAFETY VIDEO
SI Video
Box 3100
San Fernando, CA 91341
(no phone orders)
Complete information about how to make your home baby-safe.

BABYWORKS
4343 Equity Drive
Box 1667
Columbus, OH 43216
(no phone orders)
Video series on caring for baby.

FEELING FINE PROGRAMS
3575 Cahuenga Boulevard N.
Suite 440
Los Angeles, CA 90068
(213) 851-1027
Videos on pregnancy, childbirth, breast-feeding, postnatal exercise.

LOS ANGELES BIRTHING INSTITUTE
4529 Angeles Crest Highway
Suite 209
La Canada, CA 91011
(818) 952-6310
Books on childbirth and parenting.

SUPER SITTERS
Box 7020
Brick, NJ 08723
(800) 722-9999
Set of books and video to educate babysitters.

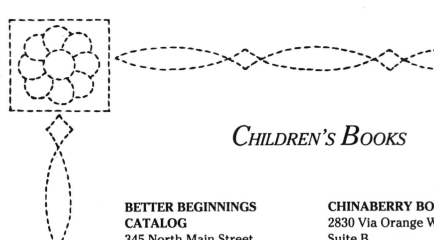

CHILDREN'S BOOKS

**BETTER BEGINNINGS
CATALOG**
345 North Main Street
West Hartford, CT 06117
(800) 274-0068;
(203) 236-4907
Books and tapes for babies and
children.

BLACKLION BOOKS
9 East Oxford Avenue
Alexandria, VA 22310
(no phone orders)
Books of all kinds for babies
and young children.

CHINABERRY BOOK SERVICE
2830 Via Orange Way
Suite B
Spring Valley, CA 92078
(800) 777-5205; (619) 670-5200
Large selection of children's
books.

GRYPHON HOUSE
Early Childhood Catalog
Box 275
Mount Rainier, MD 20712
(800) 638-0928; (301) 779-6200
Good selection of preschool
books.

**HERRON'S BOOKS
FOR CHILDREN**
Box 1389
Oak Ridge, TN 37830
(no phone orders)
Books and puzzles for young
children.

CHILDREN'S CLOTHING

AFTER THE STORK
1501 Twelfth Street N.W.
Albuquerque, NM 87104
(505) 243-9100
Complete line of cotton clothing for infants, toddlers and older children.

AT LAST, INC.
Building 32
Endicott Street
Norwood, MA 02062
(no phone orders)
Clothes for children with sizing problems. Sizes 4-14.

BABY CLOTHES WHOLESALE
70 Ethel Road West
Piscataway, NJ 08854
(908) 842-2900
Discounted infant and young children's clothing.

BIOBOTTOMS
Box 6009
Petaluma, CA 94953
(707) 778-7945
Cotton clothing and diaper covers.

BRIGHT'S CREEK
Bay Point Place
Hampton, VA 23653
(800) 622-9202; (804) 827-1850
Full line of infants, toddlers, and children's clothing.

CHILDREN'S SHOP
Box 625
Chatham, MA 02633
(800) 426-8716
High-quality clothing for babies and children.

CHILDREN'S WEAR DIGEST
Box 22728
2515 East Forty-Third Street
Chattanooga, TN 37422
(800) 433-1895
Clothing and linens for infants, toddlers, and older children.

CHOCK CATALOG CORP.
74 Orchard Street
New York, NY 10002
(800) 222-0020
Brand-name underwear, sleepwear, and socks for infants, children, and adults.

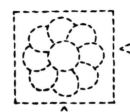

CHILDREN'S CLOTHING

CLASSICS FOR KIDS
10501 Metropolitan Avenue
Kensington, MD 20895
(301) 949-3128
Natural-fiber clothing for infants and children.

GARNET HILL
262 Main Street
Franconia, NH 03580
(800) 622-6216
Complete line of infants' and children's clothes and linens. All made of natural fibers.

HANNA ANDERSSON
1010 NW Flanders Street
Portland, OR 97209
(800) 222-0544
All-cotton clothing from Sweden. Infants, children, and mothers.

KARIN AND JOHN
525 South Raymond Avenue
Pasadena, CA 91105
(800) 626-9600
Cotton infants' and children's clothing from Sweden.

LANDS' END KIDS CATALOG
1 Lands' End Lane
Dodgeville, WI 53595
(800) 356-4444
Good-quality clothing from the people who make Lands' End adult clothing.

MAGGIE MOORE
Box 1564
New York, NY 10023
(212) 543-3434
High-quality clothing for infants and children.

OLSEN'S MILL
Highway 21
Box 2266
Oshkosh, WI 54903
(414) 685-6688
Oshkosh B'Gosh clothing for infants, children, and adults.

PATAGONIA FUNCTIONAL KIDS CLOTHES
1609 West Babcock Street
Box 8900
Bozeman, MT 59715
(800) 638-6464
All the great Patagonia outdoor wear in kids' sizes.

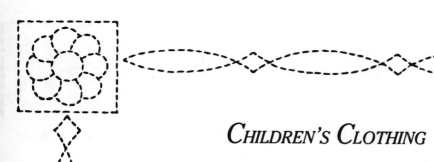

CHILDREN'S CLOTHING

PETIT PIZAZZ
2134 Espey Court No. 10
Crofton, MD 21114
(301) 858-1221
Clothing for babies and children made in the United States and Sweden.

RICHMAN COTTON COMPANY
529 Fifth Street
Santa Rosa, CA 95401
(800) 992-8924
All-cotton clothing for babies, children, and adults.

STORYBOOK HEIRLOOMS
1215 O'Brien Drive
Menlo Park, CA 94025
(800) 899-7666
Unusual dresses for girls, and some special items like rocking chairs.

THE WOODEN SOLDIER
North Hampshire Common
North Conway, NH 03860
(603) 356-7041
Unusual, charming outfits for infants, toddlers, older children—sailor suits, velvet dresses, sleepwear, etc.

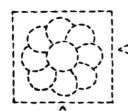

CHILDREN'S FURNITURE

BOSTON AND WINTHROP
2 East Ninety-third Street
New York, NY 10128
(212) 410-6388
Hand-painted children's furniture.

FURNITURE DESIGNS
1827 Elmdale Avenue
Glenview, IL 60025
(708) 657-7526
Furniture plans for the do-it-yourselfer. High chairs, cribs, etc.

LAURA D'S FOLK ART FURNITURE, INC.
106 Gleneida Avenue
Carmel, NY 10512
(914) 228-1440
Hand-painted folk art furniture that is functional.

J.C. PENNEY BABY AND YOU CATALOG
Catalog Distribution Center
11800 W. Burleigh Street
Box 2021
Milwaukee, WI 53201
(800) 222-6161
Wide selection of baby furniture and equipment.

SQUIGGLES AND DOTS
Box 870
Seminole, OK 74868
(405) 382-0588
Very lovely, unusual pieces.

TABOR INDUSTRIES
8220 West Thirtieth Court
Hialeah, FL 33016
(305) 557-1481
Cribs, changing tables, rocking chairs, etc.

CHILDREN'S LINEN

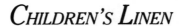

CLOUD NINE
142 Loma Alta
Oceanside, CA 92054
(619) 722-1676
Futons, sheets, comforters.

COMPANY STORE
500 Company Store Road
LaCrosse, WI 54601
(800) 356-9367
Down comforters, bumper pads.

CUDDLEDOWN
42 North Elm Street
Box 667
Yarmouth, ME 04096
(800) 323-6793; (207) 846-9781
Comforters and flannel sheets.

DOMESTICATIONS
Hanover, PA 17333
(717) 633-3333
Inexpensive sheets, quilts, and towels for children.

MONCOUR'S
4233 Spring Street
Suite 14
La Mesa, CA 92041
(800) 541-0900
Crib sheets, comforters, bumpers, quilts, etc.

PINE CREEK COMPANY
28000 S. Dryland Road
Canby, OR 97013
(503) 266-7463
Flannel crib sheets, bumper pads, comforters, etc., and some cotton baby clothing as well.

RUE DE FRANCE
78 Thames Street
Newport, RI 02840
(800) 777-0998
Lace curtains.

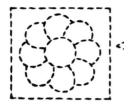

CHILDREN'S MUSIC AND VIDEO

A GENTLE WIND
Box 3103
Albany, NY 12203
(518) 436-0391
Children's musical cassettes.

ALCAZAR RECORDS
Box 429
Waterbury, VT 05676
(800) 541-9904
Distributes independent labels—
has special children's catalog.

**AUDIO THERAPY
INNOVATIONS**
Box 550
Colorado Springs, CO 80901
(800) 537-7748
Has books but also useful tapes
to lull infants to sleep.

**CHILDREN'S BOOK
AND MUSIC CENTER**
2500 Santa Monica Boulevard
Santa Monica, CA 90404
(800) 443-1856; (213) 829-0215
Large catalog of books, records,
tapes, videos, and musical
instruments.

EDUCATIONAL ACTIVITIES
Box 87
1937 Grand Avenue
Baldwin, NY 11510
(800) 645-3739; (516) 223-4666
Records, audio and videocassettes.

**EDUCATIONAL RECORD
CENTER**
1575 Northside Drive
Altanta, GA 30318
(800) 438-1637
Records, tapes, and videos
from infants to teens.

KIMBO EDUCATIONAL
Box 477
Long Branch, NJ 07740
(800) 631-2187;
(908) 229-4949
Nursery rhymes, educational
aids, on records and cassettes.

LINDEN TREE
170 State Street
Los Altos, CA 94022
(414) 949-3390
Records and cassettes of children's favorites.

MUSIC FOR LITTLE PEOPLE
Box 1460
Redway, CA 95560
(800) 346-4445
Records and cassettes by pop-
ular children's artists.

PARENTCARE LTD.
6 Commercial Street
Hicksville, NY 11801
(800) 334-3889
Wide variety of children's
videos.

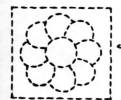

CHILDREN'S MUSIC AND VIDEO

PLAYSKOOL LULLABIES
Hasbro Direct
Box 6147
Wasterville, OH 43081
(no phone orders)
Audiocassettes personalized
with your child's name.

**SAN FRANCISCO MUSIC
BOX COMPANY**
Box 7817
San Francisco, CA 94120
(800) 227-2190; (415) 653-3022
Large selection of music boxes.

SWEET BABY DREAMS
220-F Del Vina Avenue
Monterey, CA 93940
(408) 659-3259
Lullabies and music to promote
sleep.

VID AMERICA
Box 5240
FDR Station
New York, NY 10150
(no phone orders)
Children's videocassettes.

GIFTS FOR EXPECTANT FAMILIES

**BIG BROTHER/BIG SISTER
FAN CLUB**
401 East Eighty-sixth Street
Box 214
New York, NY 10028
(212) 860-7423
When new baby arrives, older
child gets certificate, *My New
Baby and Me* book, T-shirt, etc.

DADDY'S TEES
Box 160214
Miami, FL 33116
(800) 541-7202; (305) 271-2073
Gift T-shirts for new fathers
and grandparents.

THE RIGHT START CATALOG
Right Start Plaza
5334 Sterling Center Drive
Westlake Village, CA 91361
(800) LITTLE 1
Gifts for grandparents and siblings.

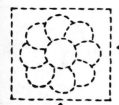

MATERNITY AND NURSING CLOTHES

BEEGOTTEN CREATIONS
Box 1800
Spring Valley, NY 10977
(800) 772-3390
T-shirts and sweatshirts for all members of the expecting family.

BOSOM BUDDIES
Box 6138
Kingston, NY 12401
(914) 338-2038
Nursing bras.

DECENT EXPOSURES
Box 736
2202 N.E. 115th Street
Seattle, WA 98215
(206) 364-4540
Nursing bras and tummy "slings."

FIFTH AVENUE MATERNITY
Box 21826
Seattle WA 98111
(800) 426-3569
High-fashion, attractive, and casual clothing, suitable for business. Nightgowns and underwear.

MOTHERHOOD
390 Sepulveda Boulevard
El Segundo, CA 90245
(310) 364-1100; (800) 421-9967
Wide range of basic maternity clothes.

MOTHER'S WORK
1309 Noble Street
Fifth Floor
Philadelphia, PA 19123
(215) 625-9259
Conservative clothing for the working woman.

PAGE BOY
8918 Governor's Row
Dallas, TX 75247
(800) 225-3103
Upbeat sportswear and business clothing.

J.C. PENNEY CATALOG
Catalog Distribution Center
11800 W. Burleigh Street
Box 2021
Milwaukee, WI 53201
(800) 222-6161
A good selection of maternity clothes.

REBORN MATERNITY
564 Columbus Avenue
New York, NY 10024
(212) 362-6965
Selections from their stores. For work and play; conservative.

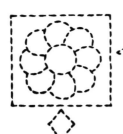

RECREATIONS MATERNITY
Box 091038
Columbus, OH 43209
(800) 621-2547;
(614) 236-1109
Selections from their stores; some-
what conservative.

NURSING SUPPLIES

BREASTFEEDING—
THE ART OF MOTHERING
Alive Productions Ltd.
Box 72
Port Washington, NY 11050
(516) 767-9235
Videotape written by a pediatrician.

LA LECHE LEAGUE
Box 1209
Franklin Park, IL 60131
(312) 455-7730
Books, breast pumps, milk stor-
age systems, breast shields.

LAIT ETTE CO.
183 Florence Avenue
Oakland, CA 94618
(415) 655-5110
Storage system for chilling and
transporting expressed milk.

LOPUCO LTD.
1615 Old Annapolis Road
Woodbine, MD 21797
(800) 634-7867;
(301) 489-4949
Hand-operated breast pumps.

MOTHER NURTURE PROJECT
103 Woodland Drive
Pittsburgh, PA 15228
(412) 344-5940
Everything you need for breast-feeding.

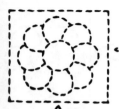

Toys and Educational Items

ABILITIES INTERNATIONAL
Old Forge Road
Elizabethtown, NY 12932
(518) 873-6456
Developmental toys and educational items.

BEAR-IN-MIND
53 Bradford Street
West Concord, MA 01742
(508) 369-1167
The best in stuffed bears.

CHILDCRAFT
20 Kilmer Road
Edison, NJ 08818
(800) 631-5657
Educational toys and games; infant toys.

CONSTRUCTIVE PLAYTHINGS
1227 East 119th Street
Grandview, MO 64030
(816) 761-5900
Good selection of infant toys, games, and toys for young children.

COYOTE COLLECTION PUZZLES
94349 Deadwood Creek Pond
Deadwood, OR 97430
(503) 964-5621
Lovely educational wooden puzzles and silkscreened wood-framed mirrors for children.

CUDDLE TOYS
PO Drawer D
Keene, NH 03431
(800) 992-9002; (603) 352-3414
High-quality stuffed animals.

EARLY LEARNING CENTRE
Box 821
Lewiston, ME 04243
(800) 255-2661
Good selection of infant and preschool toys and games.

FAO SCHWARZ
Box 182225
Chattanooga, TN 37422
(800) 426-TOYS
Fabulous toys from the famous New York toy store.

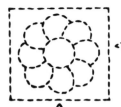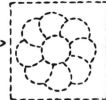

Toys and Educational Items

BACK TO BASICS TOYS
3715 Thornapple Street
Chevy Chase. MD 20815
(800) 356-5360
Many traditional and ultra-modern toys.

**FISHER-PRICE BITS
AND PIECES CATALOG**
Consumer Affairs
636 Girard Avenue
East Aurora, NY 14052
(no phone orders)
Replacement parts for
Fisher-Price toys.

GROWING CHILD
Box 620
Lafayette, IN 47902
(317) 423-2624
Toys for babies and children to age ten.

HEARTHSONG
Box B
Sebastapol, CA 95473
(800) 325-2502
Unusual toys and baby items.
Many imported.

JUST FOR KIDS
Box 29141
Shawnee, KS 66201
(800) 654-6963
Toys and games for infants, toddlers, and older children.

**LEARNING MATERIALS
WORKSHOP**
58 Henry Street
Burlington, VT 05401
(802) 862-8399
Block and construction sets.

LILLY'S KIDS
Virginia Beach, VA 23479
(804) 430-1500
Nice line of toys and educational items.

MARVELOUS TOY WORKS
2111 Eastern Avenue
Baltimore, MD 21231
(301) 276-5130
Wooden toys and block sets, well-priced.

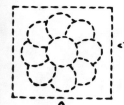

TOYS AND EDUCATIONAL ITEMS

MILL POND FARMS
Box 203
Rochester, MA 02770
(no phone orders)
Wooden toys imported from New Zealand.

PLAYFAIR TOYS
1690 Twenty-eighth Street
Boulder, CO 80301
(303) 440-7229
Good selection of infant items, toys, and games.

SESAME STREET CATALOG
2515 East Forty-third Street
Chattanooga, TN 37422
(800) 446-9415
Toys and products with all the wonderful Sesame Street characters.

TOYS TO GROW ON
2615 E. Dominguez Street
Box 17
Long Beach, CA 90801
(800) 542-8338; (213) 603-8890
Nice selection of toys and games.

WALT DISNEY KIDS CATALOG
Box 29144
Shawnee Mission, KS 66201
(800) 237-5751
T-shirts, toys, and stuffed animals with imprints from Mickey and other Disney characters.

PART SEVEN

Resources

PARENTING can be an overwhelming experience—especially in the beginning. Don't get discouraged if you feel you don't know the right answers to everything. There are many resources you can call upon for information. This section includes the following:

ORGANIZATIONS
These public and private organizations can provide you with literature and information at little or no cost.

MAGAZINES AND NEWSLETTERS
A subscription to one of the many publications for parents is a good way to get information about parenting on a regular basis.

PARENTS' GROUPS AND PRESCHOOL ACTIVITIES RECORD
You'll find there are a lot of these in your area run by churches, hospitals, schools, and private organizations. Create your own directory.

CHILD'S FRIENDS AND PARENTS
Before you know it, you'll hear about other babies in your neighborhood, or your child will make friends in a parents' group/day-care situation. You may even want to get to know the parents. Here's the place to store those names and numbers.

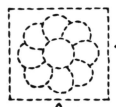

**American Academy
of Pediatrics**
Box 927
141 Northwest Point Boulevard
Elk Grove Village, IL 60009
(708) 228-5005
Has a variety of literature available, including child health record and first aid chart.

**American College of
Nurse-Midwives**
1522 K Street NW
Suite 100
Washington, DC 20005
(202) 289-0171
Can refer you to a certified nurse-midwife in your area.

**American College of
Obstetricians and
Gynecologists**
409 Twelfth Street SW
Washington, DC 20024
(202) 638-5577
Provides educational pamphlets and referral service.

American Dental Association
Department of Public Information
211 East Chicago Avenue
Chicago, IL 60611
(312) 440-2500
Literature available.

American Mothers, Inc.
The Waldorf-Astoria
301 Park Avenue
New York, NY 10022
(212) 755-2539
Dedicated to preserving family values. Sponsors local chapters and support networks.

**American Optometric
Association**
243 North Lindbergh Boulevard
St. Louis, MO 63141
(314) 991-4100
Booklets available: "Your Baby's Eyes" and "Your Pre-Schooler's Eyes."

American Red Cross
National Headquarters
Washington, DC 20006
(202) 728-6475
Local chapters sponsor infant CPR courses and other useful courses. Booklets also available.

ASPO/Lamaze
Box 952
McClean, VA 22101
(800) 368-4404; (703) 524-7802
Organization of childbirth educators who will refer you to local Lamaze instructors.

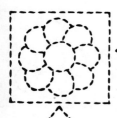

ORGANIZATIONS

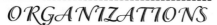

Childcare Action Campaign
99 Hudson Street
Suite 1233
New York, NY 10013
(212) 334-9595
A group dedicated to providing a national system of child care. Brochures available.

Children's Defense Fund
122 C Street NW
Washington, DC 20001
(202) 628-8787
Pays attention to the needs of poor, minority, and handicapped children. Publications available.

Child Welfare League of America
440 First Street NW
Suite 310
Washington, DC 20001
(202) 638-2952
Children's advocacy group. Books and publications available.

Circumcision Information Center
Box 765
Times Square Station
New York, NY 10108
(phone number not available)
Literature available.

Council for Interracial Books for Children
Box 1263
New York, NY 10023
(212) 757-5339
Can provide information on choosing nonracist books.

Depression After Delivery
Box 1282
Morrisville, PA 19067
(215) 295-3994
Will refer you to women who live near you and can help.

Fatherhood Project
Bank Street College of Education
610 West 112th Street
New York, NY 10025
(212) 663-7200
Provides information on subjects related to fatherhood.

Human Growth Foundation
Box 3090
Falls Church, VA 22043
(800) 451-2-6434
Free booklets and growth chart.

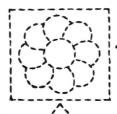

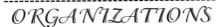

ORGANIZATIONS

International Childbirth Education Association
Box 20048
Minneapolis, MN 55420
(612) 854-8660
Has an excellent catalog of publications on childbirth, child-rearing, breast-feeding, and circumcision topics.

International Twins Association
c/o Lynn Long and Lori Stewart
6898 Channel Road NE
Minneapolis, MN 55432
(612) 571-3022
Publishes a newsletter.

Juvenile Diabetes Foundation International
432 Park Avenue South
New York, NY 10016
(800) 223-1138; (212) 889-7575
Raises funds for research and has free brochures about pregnancy and diabetes, and babies and diabetes.

La Leche League
Box 1209
9616 Minneapolis Avenue
Franklin Park, IL 60131
(708) 445-7730
Information and supplies for breast-feeding. Referrals to local chapters.

March of Dimes
1275 Mamaroneck Avenue
White Plains, NY 10605
(914) 428-7100
Literature on infant care.

National Association of the Deaf
814 Thayer Avenue
Silver Spring, MD 20910
(301) 587-1788
Catalog of publications, support groups, workshops, seminars, etc.

National Association for the Education of Young Children
1834 Connecticut Avenue NW
Washington, DC 20009
(800) 424-2460;
(202) 232-8777
Dedicated to improving services to young children and families. Books, posters, brochures.

National Association for Family Day Care
815 Fifteenth Street NW
Suite 928
Washington, DC 20005
(202) 347-3356
Organization of day-care providers, with membership open to parents. Newsletter, books available.

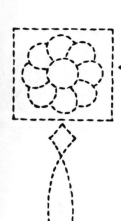

**National Association for
Parents of the
Visually Impaired**
2180 Linway Drive
Beloit, WI 53511
(800) 562-6265; (608) 362-4945
Provides support and information for parents. Several books and resource guides available.

**National Center for Learning
Disabilities**
99 Park Avenue
New York, NY 10016
(212) 687-7211
Magazine available.

**National Coalition Against
Domestic Violence**
Box 15127
Washington, DC 20003
(800) 333-7233; (202) 293-8860
Twenty-four-hour hot line provides information about shelters and programs. Working to end family violence.

**National Committee for the
Prevention of Child Abuse**
332 South Michigan Avenue
Suite 950
Chicago, IL 60604
(312) 663-3520
Organization trying to end child abuse. Free catalog of publications.

**National Down's Syndrome
Society**
666 Broadway
Suite 810
New York, NY 10012
(800) 221-4602
Provides information and local references.

National Easter Seal Society
70 East Lake Street
Chicago, IL 60601
(312) 726-6200
Books and leaflets available, for those with disabilities.

**National Federation
for the Blind**
1800 Johnson Street
Baltimore, MD 21230
(301) 659-9314
Self-help organization for the blind and visually impaired.

National Institutes for Health
Office of Communications
Editorial Operations Branch
Bethesda, MD 20892
(301) 496-4000
Free publications list on topics such as childhood hyperactivity, infantile apnea and home monitoring, baby bottle tooth decay, etc.

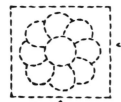

National Organization of Mothers of Twins Clubs
12404 Princess Jeanne NE
Albuquerque, NM 87112
(505) 275-0955
Coordinates local clubs. Will send free informational brochures.

National Sudden Infant Death Syndrome Foundation
10500 Little Patuxent Parkway
Suite 420
Columbia, MD 21044
(800) 221-SIDS
Provides information and local references.

Parents of Prematures
13613 NE Twenty-sixth Place
Bellevue, WA 98605
(phone number not available)
Newsletter and other literature available.

Parents of Prematures
c/o Houston Organization for Parent Education, Inc.
3311 Richmond
Suite 330
Houston, TX 77098
(phone number not available)
Has resource directory available.

Parents Anonymous
6733 South Sepulveda
Suite 270
Los Angeles, CA 90045
(800) 421-0353; (213) 410-9732
Network of self-help support groups for parents who are frightened they may hurt their children.

Parents Without Partners
8807 Colesville Road
Silver Spring, MD 20910
(800) 638-8078; (301) 588-9354
Has nine hundred local chapters and publishes a magazine.

Physicians for Automotive Safety
Box 208
Rye, NY 10580
(phone number not available)
Booklet on car seats.

Single Mothers by Choice
Box 1642
Gracie Square Station
New York, NY 10028
(212) 988-0993
An association that provides support and information to single women who are mothers or are considering it.

ORGANIZATIONS

Stepfamily Association of America
602 East Joppa Road
Baltimore, MD 21204
(301) 823-7570
Support organization for the needs of stepfamilies.

The Triplet Connection
Box 99571
Stockton, CA 95209
(209) 474-3073
For those with multiple births larger than twins. Information packets, newsletter.

U.S. Consumer Product Safety Commission
5401 Westbard Avenue
Bethesda, MD 20816
(301) 492-6800
Product safety literature.

Working Mothers Network
1529 Spruce Street
Philadelphia, PA 19102
(800) 648-8455;
(215) 875-1178
Offers seminars, workshops, newsletter, etc.

YMCA of the USA
755 W. North Avenue
Chicago, IL 60610
(312) 280-3400
Can refer you to local mother/child programs.

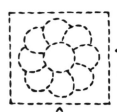

American Baby
Box 53093
Boulder, CO 80322
(800 525-0643
Offers practical advice for parents of infants.

Child Health Alert Newsletter
Box 338
Newton Highlands, MA 02161
(phone number not available)
Reports on latest findings in health-related areas for infants and children.

Child Magazine
Box 3176
Harlan, IA 51593
(800) 777-0222
Articles on parenting and a strong emphasis on children's fashion.

Exceptional Child Magazine
Parenting Your Disabled Child
605 Commonwealth Avenue
Boston, MA 02215
(phone number not available)
Informative articles for parents of children with disabilities.

Mothering Magazine
Box 1690
Santa Fe, NM 87504
(505) 984-8116
Articles on parenting approached form a holistic/naturalistic point of view.

Parents Magazine
Box 3055
Harlan, IA 51593
(800) 727-3682
The original parenting magazine features articles for parents with children of all ages.

Parenting Magazine
501 Second Street
San Francisco, CA 94107
(800) 525-0643
Useful articles on parenting for those with infants and young children.

Twins Magazine
Box 12045
Overland Park, KS 66212
(913) 722-1090
This magazine has useful information for parents of twins.

Working Mother
Box 53861
Boulder, CO 80322
(800) 525-0643
Articles are geared toward working women with families.

PARENTS' GROUPS AND PRESCHOOL ACTIVITIES RECORD

Name _____ Location _____

Date/Time _____ Phone# _____

Name _____ Location _____

Date/Time _____ Phone# _____

Name _____ Location _____

Date/Time _____ Phone# _____

Name _____ Location _____

Date/Time _____ Phone# _____

Name _____ Location _____

Date/Time _____ Phone# _____

Name _____ Location _____

Date/Time _____ Phone# _____

Name _____ Location _____

Date/Time _____ Phone# _____

Name _____ Location _____

Date/Time _____ Phone# _____

Name _____ Location _____

Date/Time _____ Phone# _____

Name _____ Location _____

Date/Time _____ Phone# _____

PARENTS' ACTIVITIES RECORD

Name _____   Location _____

Date/Time _____   Phone# _____

Name _____   Location _____

Date/Time _____   Phone# _____

Name _____   Location _____

Date/Time _____   Phone# _____

Name _____   Location _____

Date/Time _____   Phone# _____

Name _____   Location _____

Date/Time _____   Phone# _____

Name _____   Location _____

Date/Time _____   Phone# _____

Name _____   Location _____

Date/Time _____   Phone# _____

Name _____   Location _____

Date/Time _____   Phone# _____

Name _____   Location _____

Date/Time _____   Phone# _____

Name _____   Location _____

Date/Time _____   Phone# _____

Name _____   Location _____

Date/Time _____   Phone# _____

CHILD'S FRIENDS AND PARENTS

Child's name _____ Age _____

Parents' names _____ Phone# _____

Address _____

Child's name _____ Age _____

Parents' names _____ Phone# _____

Address _____

Child's name _____ Age _____

Parents' names _____ Phone# _____

Address _____

Child's name _____ Age _____

Parents' names _____ Phone# _____

Address _____

Child's name _____ Age _____

Parents' names _____ Phone# _____

Address _____

Child's name _____ Age _____

Parents' names _____ Phone# _____

Address _____

CHILD'S FRIENDS AND PARENTS

Child's name _____ Age _____

Parents' names _____ Phone# _____

Address_____

Child's name _____ Age _____

Parents' names _____ Phone# _____

Address_____

Child's name _____ Age _____

Parents' names _____ Phone# _____

Address_____

Child's name _____ Age _____

Parents' names _____ Phone# _____

Address_____

Child's name _____ Age _____

Parents' names _____ Phone# _____

Address_____

Child's name _____ Age _____

Parents' names _____ Phone# _____

Address_____

CHILD'S FRIENDS AND PARENTS

Child's name _____ Age _____

Parents' names _____ Phone# _____

Address _____

Child's name _____ Age _____

Parents' names _____ Phone# _____

Address _____

Child's name _____ Age _____

Parents' names _____ Phone# _____

Address _____

Child's name _____ Age _____

Parents' names _____ Phone# _____

Address _____

Child's name _____ Age _____

Parents' names _____ Phone# _____

Address _____

Child's name _____ Age _____

Parents' names _____ Phone# _____

Address _____

161

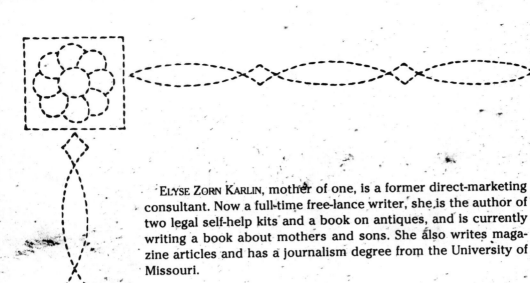

ELYSE ZORN KARLIN, mother of one, is a former direct-marketing consultant. Now a full-time free-lance writer, she is the author of two legal self-help kits and a book on antiques, and is currently writing a book about mothers and sons. She also writes magazine articles and has a journalism degree from the University of Missouri.

DAISY SPIER, mother of two, currently heads Spier Research Group, a marketing research and strategic planning firm. She has held senior positions with advertising agencies in New York. She has a bachelor's degree in psychology from McGill University in Canada, and a master's degree from Rutgers University.

MONA BRODY, mother of two, is professor of art at Bergen Community College. She has had many solo and group shows, including exhibitions in the United States and internationally. She has a B.F.A. from Moore College of Art and a master's degree in aesthetics and arts education from the Massachusetts College of Art.